Ferretir

A Traditional Country Pr

Ferreting

A Traditional Country Pursuit

David Bezzant

The Crowood Press

First published in 1998 by
The Crowood Press Ltd
Ramsbury, Marlborough
Wiltshire SN8 2HR

Paperback edition 2004

© David Bezzant 1998

British Library Cataloguing in Publication Data
A catalogue record for this book is available from the British Library.

ISBN 1 86126 706 1

Line illustrations by J. Bezzant and D. Fisher.
Photographs by D. Bezzant except those on pages 81 and 82, courtesy of
Mrs. S. Knight, Essex Ferret Welfare Society.

Typeset by Phoenix Typesetting
Ilkley, West Yorkshire

Printed and bound in Great Britain by
CPI Bath

CONTENTS

1 A TRADITIONAL COUNTRY PURSUIT

The Early Ferreters

Many people have grown up with absolutely no knowledge of the rural pastime of ferreting and when they meet characters such as myself who enthuse about little else they are justifiably curious and desire to know what the attraction might be. To relate stories of outstanding ferret action in pursuit of rabbit which fellow sportsmen would congratulate elicits a disappointingly vague response and in some cases even pity for what they consider a rather humdrum existence. Consequently, I have deduced that the best way to understand what ferreting is all about is either to go ferreting or look at the lives of the different ferreters throughout the centuries.

The first recorded activity of ferreting in Britain is from the twelfth century when both men and women of exalted social position or their employees possessed the legal right and opportunity to hunt rabbit for food and pleasure. They worked the ferret loose in conjunction with archaic purse nets placed over the exit holes of the warren and by so doing established the foundation of ferreting for centuries to come.

The Last One Hundred Years

Surprisingly, it was not until the late nineteenth century when the Ground Game Act became law that ferreting was made available to a wider population. The Act enabled tenants to hunt rabbit legally for the first time and many gave up their struggle to carve a living out of the ground and began to catch and market wild rabbit for money. Professional rabbiters, or warreners as they were known became more prolific and they would either be assigned to a large estate, rent land strewn with productive warrens or work as an itinerant travelling from one farm to another. The warrener was essentially a trapper who was also learned in the use of ferrets, terriers and lurchers. The profession exacted high demands on its participants in terms of arduous physical labour in all weathers, but in return offered independent employment, a handsome wage and considerable respect from the local populace. Although many contemporary ferreters aspire to the position of the warrener, probably because he was both a respected and expert rabbit catcher, ferreting would only have been used by him where trapping was inappropriate because it basically took too long for the man whose income was governed by the number of rabbits caught.

The most notorious figures to be associated with ferreting were that mixed bag of characters called poachers that included mischievous youths, chancers and outright scoundrels. Their motives for rebelling against legal restraint varied from lack of food to lust for money for which they were willing to risk transportation or hard labour if caught. The poacher would use the ferret because it was easily concealed, quiet and effective in operation and ensured a catch without having to return to a site for a further attempt. Consequently, the ferret was a means to an end and would often be subjected to cruel and unnecessary treatment in order to secure that end. Such treatment included blunting the incisor teeth by filing or sewing the upper and lower lips tight shut to prevent the animal killing a rabbit below ground and then remaining with it. Other poachers believed that a gentle and kind approach would provide the most useful animal for their exploits.

As rabbiting became more accessible, country dwellers applied themselves to the art of ferreting in order to provide a natural and healthy supply of meat for the table. Children growing up in rural areas had the opportunity to try their hand at ferreting or at the very least watch men laden with carrying boxes venture into the sporting field; thus, the keeping and working of ferrets began to be passed from one generation of enthusiasts to another. For some

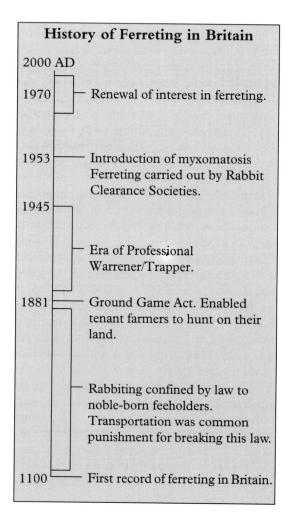

their early experience of ferreting began a life-long hobby while others chose to use it as a basis for securing country employment such as game-keeping.

Rabbiting as a profession and ferreting as a pastime suffered a severe and near fatal setback in 1953 when myxomatosis was artificially introduced to most regions of the British Isles with devastating consequences for the rabbit which underwent a rapid reduction in number of over 95 per cent. Due to this demise of the healthy rabbit, sportsmen hung up their purse nets for the last time and were not seen to venture out again except for a few of the most ardent ferreters who concentrated their efforts on locating small isolated pockets of healthy rabbits which could sustain being hunted.

During the 1970s a measured recovery in the health and number of rabbits became evident and this trend has continued up to the present time. Rabbit clearance with ferrets is once again being popularly required by landowners and practised by hunters. However, the modern ferreter defies standardized description being drawn from various walks of life, all ages and both sexes. Furthermore, we, unlike our fore-bears, have the enviable luxury of being able to work ferrets to rabbit for no other reason than enjoyment and can therefore pay due attention to the well-being of the ferret and humane management of the wild rabbit.

After a decade involved with the pastime, I adhere to the opinion that ferreting is more than catching rabbits whether it be for food or money, professionally or for pleasure. It is a living tradition of rural Britain that requires an ongoing investment of daily time and energy so that it continues to be a rewarding and interesting part of the country way of life.

A Natural Choice

Having had my expectations dashed by tenacious rabbits, my patience tried by obstinate ferrets and my body soaked and exhausted by inclement weather and unwieldy loads I have at

<table>
</table>

**Rabbit Control Methods:
Past and Present**

Traditional methods

   Ferreting

   Trapping

   Snaring

   Long-netting

   Shooting

More recent methods

   Myxomatosis

   Gassing with hydrogen cyanide

   Electric rabbit-proof fencing

Possible future methods

   Poisoned bait

   Biological means aimed at inhibiting breeding and reducing the survival rate of newly born rabbits

contribute to a successful and rewarding enterprise when hunting. As a ferreter I have derived enjoyment from access to beautiful countryside rich in wildlife and from allowing my animals to perform the function for which they were intended in such a peaceful environment, but without doubt the crowning glory of my efforts has been the provision of healthy food.

Ask any ferreter how good the ferret is at catching rabbits and he will without hesitation relate tales of productive days and large bags which clearly illustrate that the animal is as suited to its task as a duck is to water. Like all members of the weasel family, the ferret is an innate and capable predator with outstanding burrow hunting abilities, and its correct use in conjunction with purse nets has long been considered as one of, if not *the* most natural and effective means of controlling rabbits.

Like many conscientious hunters, the modern ferreter aims to hunt in a way that controls and sustains the quarry population in order to ensure its continuance and availability for other important preying animals such as buzzards, goshawks, foxes, stoats and polecats. In operation, the ferreting technique is as sporting as possible with the caught rabbit being dispatched within moments of being entangled in the purse net, or should the rabbit confound all efforts to catch it, it should escape uninjured and physically capable of maintaining its normal life.

Thankfully there is no mystery or science to the art of ferreting. It is a down-to-earth activity that has been practised successfully by both young and old, men and women. It is not exclusive, does not depend on ability or licenceship, but simply on the response of the ferrets to their keeper, the use of common fieldcraft skills plus a good supply of Job's patience. Part of the accessibility of the sport is the lack of expenditure involved in getting started and my brother acquired our first two ferrets for £1 each and a stock of twenty-five top-quality handmade purse nets for around £20. Everything else we made ourselves or requisitioned from our father's tool and garden sheds.

times wondered why anybody of sound mind and normal disposition should want to go ferreting. My puzzling is answered by the sight of a day's catch, the spectacle of ferret and dog working in unison and the taste of a well-cooked rabbit. There are a wide variety of reasons why people have chosen in the past and continue to choose to ferret, some of which are professional and others personal in nature.

Today, as at various other times, there is no necessity to go ferreting. The modern ferreter indulges in his pastime because of the enjoyment it gives which is a combination of hunting experience and the activities associated with it. These include making nets, constructing carrying boxes, finding land and obtaining permission, breeding and handling ferrets and comprehensive daily management, all of which

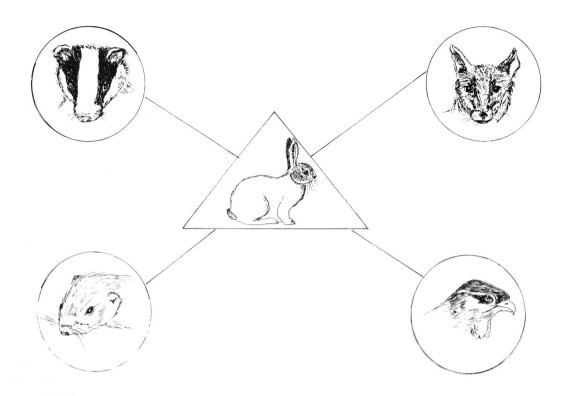

The rabbit is a valuable source of food for other wild animals such as badgers, foxes, buzzards and stoats. Following the introduction of myxomatosis these predators either turned their attention to other prey or suffered a reduction in their numbers as in the case of buzzards.

The enthusiastic gardener and lifelong farmer alike will testify to the disheartening damage that an uncontrolled wild rabbit population will inflict on crops and pastureland. For the former the annoyance emerges from the feeling that one's hard and unremitting labour has been in vain, while for the latter there is the obvious financial consideration. Both demand that something be done to reduce their losses and when my family and I lived in a rural community on the Cambridgeshire/Bedfordshire border we found that our rabbit control service was enthusiastically received and that our assurance to use the ferreting technique gained us rights denied to shooters and longdog devotees.

Throughout the past seven hundred years of ferreting each generation has realized the benefit of using a natural predator to pursue its natural quarry.

Food for the Table

Some years ago when one of our near neighbours was clearing her attic she stumbled across a stack of old editions of *Country Life* magazine dating from the late 1940s to early 1960s which she promptly offered to my mother for her perusal. In one of the earlier editions I recall an item of minor interest which gave details of how two men following the war years made their living out of ferreting and eventually earned enough money to fulfil their dream and buy a farm. Unfortunately, the economic influence of ferreting and rabbiting in general upon the lives of country dwellers is consigned to the memory and tales of a bygone era which many modern ferreters would have given their eye-teeth to experience.

The trade in wild rabbit was nationally of minimal importance in terms of revenue and when compared with farming, but in some areas such as Pembrokeshire and Anglesey, it provided the principal employment and supported ancillary rural businesses. These included ironmongers, cobblers, tailors and even watchmakers as in the case of the Pembrokeshire rabbit catchers who insisted on large waistcoat pocket watches called 'turnips' in the local vernacular and used to ensure that the trapper attended his daily meetings with the collector at the appointed time. Clothing and transport were other items of considerable expenditure and warreners were reputed to spend two to three times the usual amount for boots made to the highest standard to protect against the penetrating wetness of the morning

Reasons for Choosing Ferreting

Pest control/reduction in crop damage

Continuance of a rural tradition

Seasonal pastime that does not hunt during the rabbits' breeding season.

Natural, effective and sporting method

Enjoyable, inexpensive, non-exclusive and easy to practise irrespective of age, gender and ability

Results in the provision of healthy meat

Ethically and publicly defensible method which balances control with conservation

dew. Photographic evidence shows a variety of transport including pony and cart, donkeys, bicycles and on some rare occasions motor-bikes with the rabbits being hung over the handlebars.

For those whose purse strings were pulled tight by the national economy and low wages the rabbit appeared as manna sent from heaven with its cheap or free availability prompting a regular appearance on the dining table. At the stroke of a brush this way of life and minor rural industry was wiped out more or less overnight in order to protect the crops and economy of farmers concerned about the epidemic rise in the rabbit population and the damage they caused. Alas, the financial benefits of ferreting for the country dweller are now virtually non-existent although there are individuals who generate some extra capital from net-making and savings are made to the household economy by the procurement of free and healthy rabbit meat.

Ferreting is a natural hunting method which is a determined and controlled response to an increase in rabbit numbers and culls the popu-lation without introducing disease. Little thought was given to the pressure that the humble rabbit exerted on the British landscape and even less to what their drastic demise might cause. It was not necessary to ponder for too long because in 1953 the introduction of myxo-matosis revealed all too plainly the part that the rabbit contributed to the countryside and its flora and fauna. The rabbit was responsible for creating an environment which favoured the growth of ragwort and orchids, both of which suffered reduction as rabbits became increas-ingly scarce. Stoats and buzzards whose primary prey was the rabbit were reduced in numbers while short-eared owls, foxes and weasels flour-ished on a diet of mice and voles. Many buzzards became grossly undernourished, laid fewer eggs and experienced a greater mortality rate amongst their nestlings. Some species such as the Large Blue butterfly were lost to our shores as a direct consequence of the demise of the rabbit and the Sand Lizard was deprived of

I favour keeping my ferret cages in an outbuilding or shed because the structure will offer protection from the weather when cleaning and handling and will provide a sheltered area in which the animals can exercise. Consequently, I can spend as much time as I like with my ferrets irrespective of the weather or hour.

its prime egg-laying site previously produced by the grazing of rabbits. Whether such results are sufficient to condemn or condone the use of myxomatosis is a matter of personal opinion, but they do show that not only the farm worker felt and bewailed the loss of the rabbit, but much of nature also.

'He would rather be in his ferret shed than at work'; I have often heard it said of me and it is a truth that I cannot, nor wish to, deny for ferreting unlike work is something of which I never tire. Whether on my days off or after a day's work there is always something to be done with the ferrets and the more I do the more I want to do. My pursuit of this traditional rural pastime has influenced my perception and behaviour in the countryside and to some extent has influenced my lifestyle as a country dweller.

As ferreting is once again gaining in popularity it will continue to have consequences on the countryside and its inhabitants, and hopefully with a revival in interest in the wild rabbit for cooking will one day resume its potential for making money.

Lost Years

As a child growing up in the country I became familiar with the pitiful sight of a rabbit suffering from myxomatosis, but it was not until years later when I began ferreting that I became aware of the far-reaching consequences of the disease. The death knell for the rabbit industry was sounded, the continuance of ferreting as a field-sport was threatened and the wild rabbit was

Myxomatosis

CAUSE:
> Myxoma virus

METHOD OF SPREAD:
> *Spillopsyllus cuniculi*, the rabbit flea

INCUBATION PERIOD:
> Five days

PROGRESSION:
> Eyelids begin to swell

> Inflammation spreads to the base of the ears, forehead and nose

> Anal and genital area become swollen

> Discharge of serious fluid rich in viral material

> Death in approximately 12 days

nearly wiped out. If the beginning of the century had ushered in the golden era for rabbiting the middle of it heralded the bleakest period for the ferreter.

Myxomatosis was first mentioned in 1897 and in 1942 it was realized that the myxoma virus was naturally occuring and fatal to the European rabbit, which failed to develop immunity against it. Following the introduction of myxomatosis to the south-eastern states of Australia where annual savings of tens of millions of pounds were made, Dr Delille, a French scientist, introduced the virus to his enclosed estate near Paris. The virus refused to be contained and by June of 1942 98 per cent of wild rabbits in France were dead. The powerful hunting and sporting lobby went after Delille in the law courts; he meanwhile spoke before the Académie d'Agriculture supporting the systematic use of myxomatosis for the control of wild rabbits. Rabbit hunters and fanciers were alike disgusted when Delille triumphed in the law courts and received a gold medal from the Académie for his endeavours.

In 1953 myxomatosis, transported by a migratory bird, crossed the Channel into Sussex and Kent. In 1954 myxomatosis spread to the rest of England, Wales, Scotland and Ireland, but this time it was transported by man. The massive reduction in rabbit numbers resulted in savings of £30–50m for foresters and farmers whose crops had previously suffered from overpopulation, but the general public was outraged at the hideous appearance of suffering rabbits, and farm and rural workers were annoyed with those who were robbing them of their traditional meat supply.

Consequently, the rabbit became an object of pity which few wanted to hunt and even less wanted to eat. The ferreter had little if any incentive to venture out and there remained no need for landowners to grant them access any longer, but myxomatosis was not the only reason for the decline in ferret keeping and working. Other influential factors include altered lifesyles, work patterns and leisure activities combined with a modern philosophy that embraces anti-fieldsport feeling and believes hunting to be a waste of time when meat can be bought so readily.

The ferret has also suffered from the perpetuation of myths regarding its behaviour and has been dogged by a poor public image which trivializes the animal and its function as a hunter. Indiscretions with teeth and barbaric behaviour committed by a minority of ill-advised owners have been recounted with such vigour that ferrets are commonly thought to be evil animals kept by bad men. As many visitors to my ferret shed have found out to their surprise ferrets can be completely tamed and are full of character and do not at all conform

The adult hob is between 40–60cm long from head to tail and weighs from 3–5lb. Jills are shorter in length and less in weight, and sexual diamorphism is a familiar feature of most mustelids

to their previously held misconceptions.

Although the modern ferreter may never experience the catches of pre-myxomatosis days, a rise in rabbit numbers and willingness by landowners to accept the ferreting method to control them means that the lost years are now well and truly behind us. The ferret is once again recognized as a useful working animal with a viable purpose in our contemporary rural environment.

2 THE FERRET

An Uncertain Past

Despite the combined efforts of scientists and naturalists engaged in intricate anatomical measurements and detailed observation of ferret behaviour the ferreter is no closer to knowing the origin of his humble creatures than he was years ago. My collection of books on ferrets propose various origins dependent upon the author's preference, but as one astute writer suggests, the origin of ferrets, like their history, must remain a secret hidden by time.

One of the earliest theories to emerge put forward the view that the ferret is a domesticated version of the Asiatic polecat which is easily tamed and shares a similar appearance to many of our modern ferrets. Others agree that the ferret is essentially a polecat, but of the European and not the Asiatic kind. The evidence for their view is the close relationship between the size and shape of the two animals' anatomy together with their ability to inter-breed. Finally, there is the old countryman's belief that the ferret is a product of crossing tame stoats and polecats which had been taken from the wild because of their ability to hunt rabbits. Following selectivity and hybridization over many years a standardized animal that bred true is supposed to have emerged and became known as the ferret.

The history of the domestication of the ferret is equally uncertain. The earliest date that I have come across is 3000BC which means that the Egyptians must have found a use for the ferret if this is to be believed. It is agreed that ferrets of a sort were used in Roman times, but there is nothing to tell us whether the Latins had found the animal in use amongst people over whom they had been victorious. Others suggest that domestication came later under the guiding hand of the Normans and many historians believe that from the eleventh to the thirteenth centuries the Crusaders brought working ferrets to Europe where they probably bred with the European polecat.

This web of historical confusion is one which I am incapable of disentangling and to be honest, even if answers could be conclusively provided, I doubt whether they would make an iota of difference to any ferreter's outlook. The general information which has been plain to observant countrymen for centuries has proved enough to inform our daily management and working expectations of the ferret. They caught fleeting glimpses of weasels, stoats and polecats and realized that the ferret bore such a similarity of conformation and behaviour that it must surely belong to the same family.

The family to which weasels and polecats belong is called *Mustelidae* and comprises a mixed bag of characters who enjoy a wide range of habitats in all parts of the world with the exception of Antarctica and Australasia, although they have been introduced into New Zealand. This family includes the mink, pine marten, wolverine, skunk, otter, badger and honey badger. In appearance they all share a short-legged, long-bodied design which is modified to suit the environments in which they live and the animals upon which they prey.

The ferret belongs to a sub-family of the *Mustelidae* which is called the *Mustelinae* and has for its closest relatives the weasel, stoat,

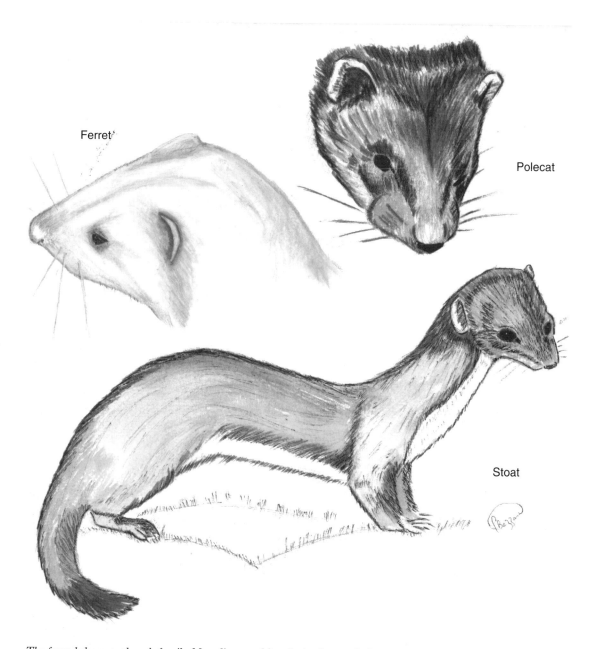

Ferret

Polecat

Stoat

The ferret belongs to the sub-family Mustelinae and has for its closest relatives the polecat and the stoat.

polecat and mink, most of which make their homes in the hollowed-out bases of old trees. Polecats will establish and patrol a range of anything between a couple of hundred and a few thousand acres and as solitary animals will mark the boundary of their territory. Although they generally avoid confrontation with one another they are such prolific and efficient hunters that they have gained a reputation as the bandits of the hedgerows and together with weasels will prey upon small rodents, rabbits, birds, insects, lizards and frogs. They are capable of catching animals far in excess of their own size and people say that a stoat will instil such an uncanny sense of hopelessness in the heart of the rabbit which it is pursuing, that the victim will literally become frozen with terror and surrender itself. These mustelids kill by sinking their teeth into the nape of their victims and thereby severing the spinal cord at the base of the cranium.

It is little wonder that the men who witnessed these smallest of carnivores at work were tempted to try their hand at taming them for their own purpose and, fortunately for the ferreter, their early attempts were so successful that the ferret was soon established as an intelligent working animal for the hunter of rabbits. There can be little doubt in the minds of those who have witnessed the effect of a ferret unleashed upon a warren that the ancestor of the ferret was domesticated because of this fundamental talent for catching rabbits.

Appearance

On a cool autumnal evening as I was dunking the last round of bread into the rich yolk of a newly laid egg I watched with interest as a figure clad in plus-fours presented my brother with two long-awaited and much-spoken-about ferrets. I was particularly curious because unlike my brother who had done some rabbiting in his younger days I had never had the opportunity to observe a ferret closely. I must confess that I did not know exactly what to expect and having introduced my ferrets to members of the public it is obvious that neither do they. Over the years I have had the opportunity to observe a host of different ferrets and the following description of the appearance of the ferret in normal health is a summary of my general thoughts about the conformation of the animals.

Ferrets enjoy a variety of sizes and colour depending upon such factors as their sex, breeding and management. The first hob and jill that we kept showed that familiar feature of the mustelid, referred to as sexual diamorphism, in which the male markedly exceeds the size of the female. However, I have noted the

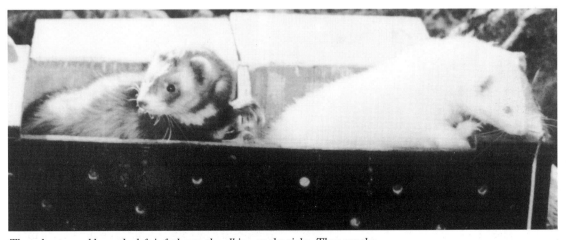

The polecat or sable on the left is father to the albino on the right. They are the most common examples of the domesticated ferret and differ only in their coat and eye colour. Suggestions of essential differences in ability and character between the sable and albino are dubious hypotheses.

An albino. Albinism in the ferret is considered as a desired characteristic and not an inherited disorder. The albino ferret is full of vigour and perfectly equipped for the role of rabbiting.

occurrence of large jills and small hobs which are very nearly the same size, but in all such cases the two animals do not share the same parentage and when placed side by side with their littermates the familiar pattern of diamorphism reappears. There are two explanations offered for the large difference in size between the male and female mustelid. The first is that they will select different animals to prey upon and so avoid competing against one another for food while the second suggests that males who compete with one another for love and land have developed a larger size based upon sexual selection so that they might be better equipped to fight for what they want. In the world of the mustelid, the bigger you are, the more dominant and powerful you become.

Although sizes may vary, all ferrets have the same basic shape which is shared by other members of the weasel family and most noticeably by the stoat and polecat. The ferret possesses a long lithe body set on short legs, has a wedge-shaped head set upon a thick neck at one end and a tail measuring approximately half its body length at the other, and in between the two a long vertebral column that results in

The ferret has a broad neck of incredible strength which helps it to fasten onto its prey with an unrelenting hold.

The fur of the ferret consists of long guard hairs projecting from a soft undercoat and is silky to touch. This ferret has a summer coat that is closer to the body and less dense than the lavish winter coat that is accompanied by an increase in subcutaneous fat.

the characteristic arching of the back in the mid-section.

It used to be said that there were two varieties of ferret, the polecat and the white or albino. Many of the people who ask me questions about my ferrets all too often believe that these are two separate animals rather than the same animal in different clothing and they are surprised to see the wide variety of colours in which the ferret appears. I have kept three different colours ranging from the traditional white-coated albino with its red eyes to the dark sable polecat with its familiar mask. The third is a pleasant compromise between the two bearing the characteristic markings of the polecat, but with a lighter coat that is referred to by the Americans as a butterscotch. A further six colour variations of the ferret are listed in America. These are:

1. The black-eyed white that shares the same coat as the albino, but with eyes as black as the ace of spades.
2. The silver-mitt which has a silver sheen to its coat, black eyes, a white blaze on its chest and four white feet.
3. The cinnamon with its black eyes and white undercoat crowned with light cinnamon guard hairs is very thin on the ground and at present peculiar to breeders in America.
4. The sterling silver resembling the silver mitt, but with a ligher more ghostly topcoat.
5. White-footed butterscotch which has the characteristic white flash on the chest and the white feet of the silver mitt, but the colour of the butterscotch.

The characteristic masked head of the polecat which also has black eyes, a brown nose and cream ear tips.

A lighter shade of polecat known as the butterscotch which has sand-coloured guard hairs. Note the darker colour of the legs and tail of this ferret.

6. Spotted, which I have never seen and only heard of. They are obviously very rare and are supposed to have spotted markings on the belly.

Whatever the colour of the ferret, the make-up of the coat is essentially the same consisting of a foundation layer of soft close hair through which projects longer coarse guard hair. The functions of the coat are to protect the skin from ultraviolet light, extremes of temperature and also from fauna. Muscle fibres present in the dermal layer of the skin enable the hairs of a ferret to be held perpendicular to the body surface and, consequently, a deep layer of insulating air is held next to the skin which prevents heat loss. The erection of hair, known as horrip-ilation, is used by the ferret as a canny weapon of defence by creating the illusion of it being fearsomely larger than it really is and so frightening off its enemies by its appearance alone. Finally, the coat acts as a tactile or sensory organ due to the presence of peripheral nerve endings around hair follicles.

Although many writers and ferret keepers have asserted that albinos and polecat-ferrets differ in character from one another, I have failed to find any standardized difference that commonly exists between the two and believe that a reliance on coat colour is a most dubious method for determining the behaviour of an intelligent animal.

The primary tools of the ferret are its eyes, ears, nose, mouth and paws. The eyesight of the

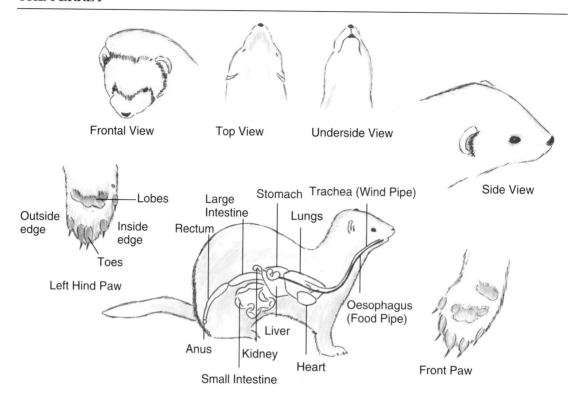

Frontal View

Top View

Underside View

Side View

Lobes

Outside edge

Inside edge

Toes

Left Hind Paw

Large Intestine

Stomach

Trachea (Wind Pipe)

Lungs

Rectum

Oesophagus (Food Pipe)

Anus

Liver

Kidney

Heart

Small Intestine

Front Paw

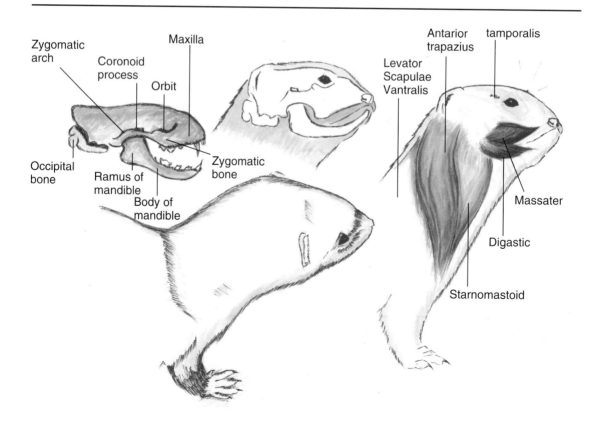

Zygomatic arch

Coronoid process

Maxilla

Orbit

Occipital bone

Ramus of mandible

Body of mandible

Zygomatic bone

Antarior trapazius

tamporalis

Levator Scapulae Vantralis

Massater

Digastic

Starnomastoid

Opposite page, upper:
The arrangement of the major organs of the ferret and the typical presentation of the paws, each having five digits. The head of the ferret has a characteristic wedge or triangular shape, whether viewed from above, beneath or the side.

Opposite page, lower:
The muscle culture of the neck equips the ferret with remarkable strength for its size.

Below:
The skeletal system of the ferret showing the long vertebral column.

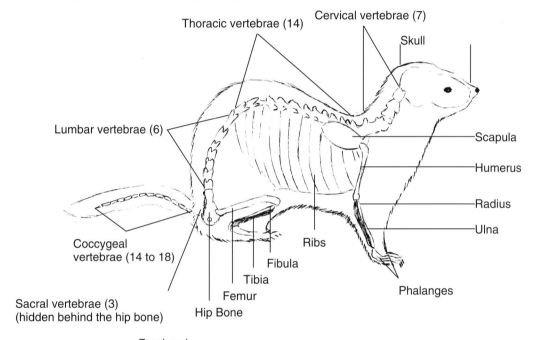

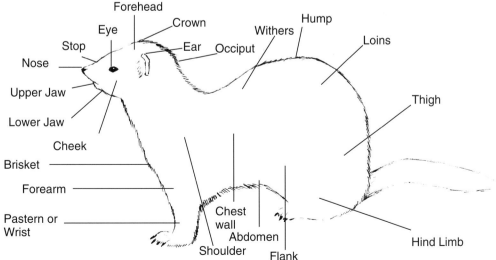

The points of the ferret highlighting the most common characteristics.

ferret is generally considered to be reasonably poor as the animal suffers from a degree of myopia (short-sightedness). However, I have noticed among my own ferrets that some of them display a greater acuity of vision or make better use of this poorly developed sense than others. One of my jills called Sally literally wanders about with her head in the clouds and never appears to be looking where she is going while another jill named Squealor shows a determined concentration as she surveys all that falls within her optical field of view. The ferret has two forward-facing eyes which can be either red or black in colour and are contained within the optical orbits of the cranium. Ferrets do not see as well in bright light as they do in dim light and they appear to have a slightly delayed focusing time.

Fortunately, the ferret has more than its eyes to rely on and uses its ears with great proficiency during everyday activities and when hunting. The ferret's ear consists of the ear flap which is held erect, forward facing and finely covered with hair, the external ear canal, middle ear and internal ear. These determine the hearing, balance and posture of the animal. The sight of a stoat sitting upright in an attitude of intense

listening illustrates the fact that they hunt very largely by their sense of hearing and are capable of discerning direction and distance by such means. The ferret hunts in the same manner, although, if you have ever attempted to wake a snoring ferret from its deep slumber, you would never believe that its hearing is one of its finest honed senses.

The ferret explores its surroundings more by smell than sight and the keeper will notice the head of the ferret moving this way and that along the ground as the nose relays messages to the brain. The nose is either pink or brown in colour depending upon the coat colour, is situated at the end of the snout and is plastic in feel.

The mouth is the most commonly spoken-about and feared part of the ferret's anatomy because it contains an impressive and savage set of teeth that are treated with suspicion by nervous onlookers. For the ferret and its relatives the arrangement and appearance of such teeth are vital to their survival by enabling them to kill their prey with consummate skill. The ferret's set of teeth consists of three kinds which are the incisors, set in the anterior or front of the mouth, the canines, set immediately behind the incisors and the molars, set behind the canines.

An elderly polecat hob showing the arching of the back – a common feature of mustelids that share the design of a long body set upon short legs.

The ferret possesses an alert and confident expression.

The canines are used for holding onto and killing prey, while the incisors and molars are used for tearing and crushing the carcass. It is the canines with their long needle-like projections that generally make people wary of ferrets and if one has the misfortune to have a finger bitten by one a wound of approximately 6mm depth can be expected. The upper canine teeth are the strongest and there is a small space between them and the corner incisor teeth in which the lower set of canines are situated when the mouth is closed. In conjunction with their impressive teeth, ferrets have strong jaws and necks which enable them to hold onto and drag burdens exceeding their own size and weight.

At the base of its short legs the ferret has feet or paws, each of which has a separated pad and five toes. Projecting from each toe is a non-retractable claw which can be used for gripping and climbing and when hunting and fighting. The pad is hairless and pink and the paws of the front legs are used more skilfully than the rear feet. The ferret will also use its feet for such activities as digging and nest-building.

An important feature of the ferret's anatomy are the anal glands which consist of two groups of skin glands, each of which empties into a storage sac which opens via a sphincter near the anus. The foul-smelling contents contained within these sacs may be discharged, either

The ferret is capable of balancing on its hind legs in similar fashion to stoats so that it can survey its surroundings.

voluntarily, to mark territory, in which case only a small amount of fluid is secreted, or as a reflex action in times of severe stress when a larger quantity is secreted as a weapon of defence.

The ferret has a handsome apperance, wears an alert and confident expression and possesses an anatomical outline which betokens its ability as a burrow hunter. However, in order to fulfil its commission by man the ferret must also display a level of intelligence and suitable instinctive and learnt behaviour.

Behaviour

The recent screening of a programme on television regarding a study of the ways and wiles of stoats opened the eyes of many viewers to the immense character that is contained within their little bodies. Even the cameraman confessed to being captivated by their mischievous behaviour, eventful excursions, independent air and happy expressions. Behaviourally, the ferret differs very slightly from stoats, weasels

The ferret during play, at rest and feeding.

and polecats and those differences that are noticeable are due to the role of domestication placed upon and enjoyed by the ferret. It did not take me long to realize that the ferret is a lively, confident and intelligent animal with a repertoire of idiosyncratic behaviour that makes it a pleasure to keep and hunt with, although admittedly some ferret antics will exasperate the average mortal, as my brother and I can testify.

The influential forces that combine to shape a ferret's behaviour are inherited characteristics, the treatment bestowed upon the animal by its keeper and the environment in which it lives. These will determine its behaviour towards other animals and man and must be understood in order for the ferreter to get the best out of his animals.

As a member of arguably the fiercest family of carnivores, the ferret has inherited an instinct for hunting and killing that is both strong and ruthless, accounting for many facets of its typical character such as determination, obstinacy, curiosity and concentration – all qualities used by hunting animals to stalk, catch and hold onto their prey. The tenacity that can be expected of the ferret is illustrated by the hunting exploits of its wild relatives that have been observed by naturalists and countrymen alike who provide us with records of particular interest. There were forty years ago a number of documented

My ferrets enjoy exercising in the stone shed and clambering over bales of hay.

A hob and jill showing their innate curiosity as they enjoy exploring every nook and cranny during their daily period of free exercise.

cases describing how weasels that attacked pheasants secured such a hold that they would not let go of the prey even when it rose to the air in an effort to rid itself of the fearsome torturer. Having flown a short distance the pheasant generally fell dead to the earth with the little antagonist still holding tight. There were other similar records of weasels cleaving fast onto hares as they thundered across the ground. Not surprisingly the ferret shows the same dogged determination when making its way through the long twisting tunnels of a warren in pursuit of rabbit.

As a territorial hunting animal the ferret will be protective of and patrol what it has established as its own domain and has a huge capacity for exercise. It will also play-fight or practise the killing movement with members of its social

Jills tends to have more compact bodies and pointed faces than hobs.

Ferrets will wrestle with one another for long periods during which time the young will practise and hone their fighting and hunting skills.

group, but because the need to hunt is eliminated by the provision of food, the ferret will expend its energy on every playful method that it can imagine.

The ferret's instinct is so powerful that if left to its own devices it would manifest a semi-wild pattern of behaviour and so must be handled by its keeper from an early age in order to become accustomed to human company. When a kind and appropriate system of managing the ferret is implemented on a daily basis the owner will realize the animal's capacity for reciprocating his care and regard. A ferret that has been properly tamed will be friendly, totally reliable regarding not biting and actually show signs of enjoying the company of its owner. In my experience ferrets are generally happy animals that are quite quickly tamed. I have also found that my ferrets will accept the company of my dog and play and work with her willingly even though they did not grow up together and I base my success fundamentally on making sure that my ferrets are first docile with me and then exposing them gradually to my dog. I also keep poultry, fowl and birds of prey and would not let the ferrets within a mile of them because the ultimate outcome would be obvious. When placed in a situation with prospective prey species the ferret's instincts will ignite with veritable blood-lust, particularly where chickens are concerned.

Although ferrets will develop working relationships with dogs, they should be kept well away from livestock and especially chickens. Even this captive-bred barn owl needs to be flown and kept at a great distance from the ferrets.

The Language of Ferrets

Like most animals, the ferret has a method of communicating its enjoyment and more obviously annoyance with a person, situation or another animal. The ferret is an expressive animal and is sensitive to kind or cruel behaviour which will inspire or diminish the spectrum of communicative action manifested. Ferrets have many ways of telling their keeper that they are fed up with their attention, want to play or are about to commit murder if they are not left alone. The ferret has the ability to communicate audibly, will use a repertoire of body movements and can resort to the more primitive and direct messages made plain by biting. The keeper should be aware of how his animals communicate in order to assess their happiness with a situation and foresee their behaviour. Although ferrets have a common appearance and express themselves in fundamentally the same way it must not be forgotten that they are individuals and possess their own characters, which is made plain by reliance on a dominant feature or method of communicating. Consequently, the keeper will find that some of his animals are persistent chatterers, while others are more apt to jump and dance about.

I have noticed three different sounds intoned by my ferrets quite regularly that are correspondingly accompanied by the same behaviour each time they are produced and, therefore, can be quite accurately interpreted. The most obvious audible sound made by the ferret is that of shrieking which is clearly an expression of pain and distress as anybody who has unwittingly stood upon the tail of one of his animals will testify. If a ferret is being overpowered by a bullying, aggressive or over-playful hob, it is also likely to shriek to let the world know that it has had enough and either wants help or to be left alone. If the keeper hears loud shrieking that persists he should definitely investigate in order to ensure that the animal is not in pain. However, it is worth remembering that ferrets can be rather sensitive and will use their shriek unashamedly.

The ferret can be observed chuntering away to itself in a constant clamour as it searches out new ground or investigates known territory. This relates to an assertion of its territorial security, delivers a cautious message of its presence and may act as an appeal to other ferrets to show themselves. This persistent humming is most evident when the ferrets are first released from their cages and commence their routine investigation of the shed combining it with the sensory information relayed by the nose.

The final sound, which is unmistakable wherever there are happy ferrets, is a vibrant 'chub-bub-bub' sound almost sung out and is most commonly observed accompanied by ecstatic jumping and dancing and endeavours to arouse play in those ferrets in closest proximity.

As in man, the body of the ferret is used as an expressive tool and can display welcoming, defensive or aggressive behaviour. When defensive or afraid the ferret fans out the hair of its body and tail giving the impression that it is larger than it actually is.

The most instinctive tool of communication of the mustelid is the mouth with its unnervingly sharp teeth that are most commonly used to show displeasure or aggression. The mouth is used to test new objects and ward off those in whom the ferret is not confident. However, a well-tamed ferret will enjoy mouthing the hand of the keeper in play without breaking the skin in much the same way as a dog.

It is a peculiar feature of the ferret that the back of the neck is more thickly covered with hair, develops faster and is used throughout the life-cycle when ferret communicates with like. From its early days the mother uses the back of the neck to transport an escaping kit back into the heart of the nest. As the kits grow they like to seize the back of the neck in play as if a ritual of practice for the future and sure method of exciting reciprocal action from their littermates. As the ferrets mature into adulthood the neck is prominent in the mating process. The hob will seize and drag the jill, upon whom he lavishes his attention, unceremoniously about. All of these various holds upon the neck at different stages throughout the lifespan have a very specific meaning. The first is that of correction, discipline and maternal protection. The second is to tantalize into play and practice the combat manoeuvre for killing while the third induces ovulation. The neck of the ferret is one of the most developed tools of its receptive communication and can be used effectively by the keeper for discipline and control. Beyond these specific communicative tools, the ferret makes its feelings known by the look in its eyes and expression on its face and the keeper who is familiar with

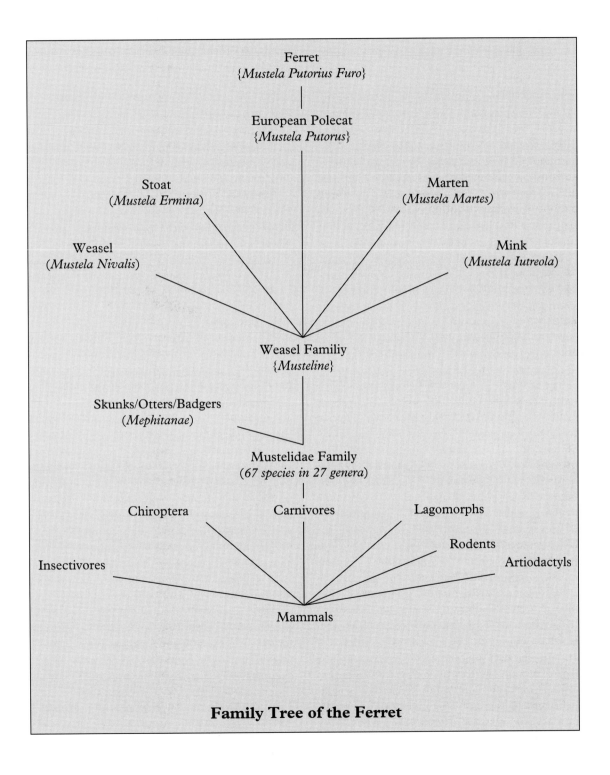

Ferret
{*Mustela Putorius Furo*}

European Polecat
{*Mustela Putorus*}

Stoat
(*Mustela Ermina*)

Marten
(*Mustela Martes*)

Weasel
(*Mustela Nivalis*)

Mink
(*Mustela Iutreola*)

Weasel Familiy
{*Musteline*}

Skunks/Otters/Badgers
(*Mephitanae*)

Mustelidae Family
(*67 species in 27 genera*)

Chiroptera   Carnivores   Lagomorphs

Rodents

Insectivores

Artiodactyls

Mammals

Family Tree of the Ferret

his animals will be able to accurately interpret their gestures.

Training

At our local annual agricultural show, I was delighted to find an antiquarian bookstall that contained a copy of *Live Stock of the Farm,* Volume VI published in 1916, in which a contributor named Edward Ash had written a short, but very interesting chapter on ferrets and their management. I first encountered his work over ten years ago when my brother told one of our near neighbours that we were thinking of getting some ferrets. Without further ado, the neighbour went into his house and returned clutching a well-kept copy of the book which had guided his ferret-keeping as a lad. Consequently, many of our expectations and thoughts about the ferret were influenced by the wisdom that the writer had gained from his many years of ferret-keeping.

Mr Ash is of the opinion that the most fascinating part of keeping ferrets is probably their training and he claimed that the ferret is one of the most intelligent animals in existence, comparable possibly with the dog. Modern research has shown that the ferret has definite powers of retention and is comparable to primates in performance.

Our first two albinos came via a gamekeeper from a boy owner who had lost much of his initial enthusiasm for the creatures and left them very much to fend for themselves. Our near neighbour who had lived in the countryside all his life and had fond memories of ferrets from his childhood came round to give his opinion of them. It was short, but definitely not sweet as he matter-of-factly stated that they would never amount to anything. His assessment was not based upon their physical condition, for although looking rough they did not appear to have acutely degenerated, but upon their uninhibited hostility towards all efforts at handling. It became obvious to us that if we hoped to reap any benefit, either in terms of working them to

rabbit or of pleasurable ownership, they would have to undergo some form of training, for a ferret left to its own devices or merely fed is neither useful nor ornamental. Consequently, the intention of training is to:

1. Tame the ferret.
2. Ensure that its instincts for rabbiting can be used in accordance with man's hunting endeavours.
3. Make the ferret a biddable and useful animal to own.

There are three methods or processes of training which are relevant to the keeper and these are:

1. Encouraging and reinforcing desired behaviour.
2. Through exercise.
3. With food.

In an ideal situation training should commence at an early age, preferably four to six weeks if the jill is compliant. The keeper should regularly and gently handle the kits and by repeated exposure so familiarize himself with the litter that his skin is readily accepted without first being nipped. A young kit will test objects with its teeth including the hands of the keeper in which case he must be tolerant and continue to handle the ferret calmly. As a puppy does, the kit soon learns that it serves no purpose to bite a kind hand. Given the correct amount of time and attention the sane ferret should be reasonably trustworthy at around eight to ten weeks, although in my experience I have found that different kits respond at a varying pace and thought should be given to the individuality of the animal's character as it delvelops. The emphasis of successful training is to get to know and be known by your animal and, on the basis of a kind and attentive relationship, to expect the fruits of tame and useful behaviour.

The old ferret keepers always used to make a certain sound as they approached the cage of the ferret when it was feeding time. As any contemporary keeper will tell you, the ferret anticipates its food with some pleasure and by making the same sound day after day the ferret learns to make the association. Although this noise will not cause the ferret to return to the keeper in the same way as a well-trained dog, it will be adequate to arrest the attention of a wandering ferret and some of my animals are quite reliable at coming to my feet when I give out the familiar call. Mr Ash claims that he used to take ten-week-old youngsters out for walks and by calling them when they were about to stray and allowing them to catch hold of a decoy in the shape of a piece of rabbit, they behaved better than any pup. He used also to introduce his ten-week-olds to a dead rabbit and would vigorously shake it at them so that they would develop a keen grip. Young kits can be allowed with the mother jill down a small warren where the mother's presence will encourage them to go into and return from the underground tunnels. If a rabbit is bolted it should be dispatched and left at the mouth of the exit hole so that the young ferrets can experience the rewards of their labour.

There are various opinions on whether a ferret actually needs training for its purpose or whether it will instinctively perform what is required of it. Admittedly, no ferret needs teaching how to hunt rabbits in the twisting cavernous tunnels of the warren, but the animal must learn how to use this talent in conjunction with the weapons and handling of man. An untrained ferret is by no means a pleasure and the better tamed and more responsive the animal, the more useful it is and the more agreeable its company, the happier also is the animal itself.

In the taming and training of the ferret I do not favour an aggressive or punishing approach and disagree with the practice of forcing a finger in the mouth of a biting ferret in order to discourage its behaviour. Not only is this uncomfortable and potentially dangerous to the structure of the mandible, but there is doubt as to its real and lasting effectiveness. If the keeper must discipline the ferret he should take a lesson from its mother and give it a firm shake of the neck and leave it at that. The ferret is not an animal to be hit and bullied to make it conform. In my experience I have found that the keys to taming and training ferrets are:

1. Daily contact with the animals during which time they can be handled.
2. A confident calm approach at all times is more constructive than punishment.
3. Patience with the ferret. Expectations of the animal should be moderated and time allowed for the animal to mature and develop.

The ferret is instinctively and anatomically designed for burrow hunting and has the intelligence to be taught how to use these abilities according to the desires of the rabbit-hunting man and in such a way as to make them a pleasurable and interesting animal to work and own.

3 FERRET MANAGEMENT

Daily Needs and Requirements

In the small Cambridgeshire village in which I used to live, my brother held a position of local notoriety owing to his ferret keeping and rabbiting endeavours and consequently enjoyed the company of other like-minded field-sportsmen. One of his acquaintances, a part-time fireman and ironmonger, expressed an interest in ferrets and procured two small albinos from a country market. A month or two passed before, in response to my brother's enquiry, he was informed that the ferrets had been shot because of their aggressive behaviour and failure to improve. Eager to find out more, my brother questioned him further and discovered that the animals had been fed irregularly and not always daily, had been cleaned infre-

quently and denied access to daily exercise beyond the cage walls. Whilst not malicious, my brother's acquaintance through ignorance of the ferrets' needs had established an inadequate and cruel regime that resulted in the premature and needless death of his animals.

Just because the ferret is a working animal does not mean that it can care for itself. A working animal must receive as much attention as a pet and arguably more for the demands placed upon its shoulders are far greater. The ferret thrives on daily contact, requires a well-planned and regular diet and relishes the opportunity to exercise beyond the boundaries of its cage. Ferrets soon become used to a routine and will anticipate the arrival of the keeper, whether it be to clean their cage or offer them food. The ferret benefits from daily care

Ferrets are gregarious animals and relish the opportunity to play with one another.

This jill is displaying her ability to dig in an effort to expose the hob who is hiding below our makeshift wooden step.

Having achieved her objective the jill joins the hob beneath the step and quickly makes him exit.

The long vertebral column and short legs of the ferret enable it to move in and out of tight spaces making it ideal for burrow hunting.

in terms of its health, well-being and content-ment and the foundation for success when hunting is laid during this time.

I spend a minimum of an hour a day involved in the routine care of my ferrets during which time my attention is given to exercising the crea-tures, cleaning the environment in which they live and providing them with appropriate food. Each of these activities will now be discussed separately so that the reader may realize the ease with which they may be carried out and their importance for the ferret.

The Importance of Exercise

Exercise is important because it keeps an animal fit and happy and provides the opportunity for it to enact ritual behaviour in play as well as get

used to being handled by its keeper. I have noticed two constantly manifested responses by my ferrets to release from the confines of the cage. The first is an investigatory search of familiar territory taken at a methodical pace akin to the businesslike approach displayed when entering a rabbit warren. The second type of movement is unrestrained bounding and so called dancing in which the ferret will jump from the floor, twist and turn in mid-air and more often than not leap on top of another ferret engaged in the same activity or dash for cover at full speed as soon as its feet return to the ground. As ferrets are animals that never seem to grow up, they will continue in such play until they become physically tired. These antics which have to be seen to be appreciated clearly

The European polecat will range over 200 to 6,000 acres depending on how rich the habitat is in prey and whether it is the breeding season or not. This jill is investigating what she considers her familiar territory.

express the animal's delight at being released from its cage.

My ferrets always begin their exercise on the floor of the ferret shed where they can safely rout about for some time. When they start to get bored with the ferret shed, I simply open the gate which allows them access to a large rough outside area where they can roll in the long grass and feel for themselves the full effects of the weather. Whilst exercising freely outside my ferrets need to be watched constantly. Some will exercise in the immediate locality and return to the shed while others are of a more wandering nature and will soon be out of sight. Many people have asked me whether my ferrets would return to their home if left to their own devices, but this is a hypothetical question that cannot be safely tested due to the risk to the ferret's health should it decide to stay away, not to mention the destruction that a loose ferret can incur on the local poultry and pet population.

One of the favourite places of interest for my ferrets is the stone workshop adjoining the ferret shed where they can roam freely and ascend and descend the various features that it contains.

Ferrets will readily climb and consequently thought should be given to the placement of objects to eliminate the risk of falling.

Exercise runs, built on an ark principle, are beneficial for containment or if you have time restrictions. If these conform to the correct dimensions they will provide an area in which the animal can progress through a full range of movements. The only detrimental aspect of relying on this form of exercise is the propensity of the ferret to curl up and go to sleep because of the confinement. Runs lack the continual stimulation that ferrets experience when

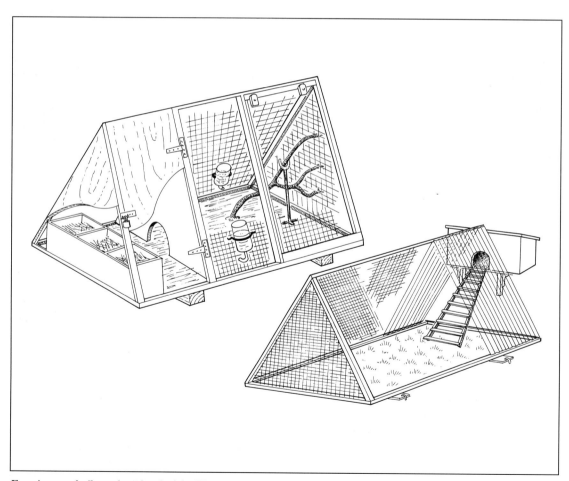

Exercise runs built on the ark principle. The run should be made secure by making a wire or wooden floor and it is worth including a sheltered area by incorporating corrugated plastic or wood into the design.

During the summer months I will take a ferret with me as I walk the dog round the fields and allow the ferret to wander about in the long grass.

unrestrained and self-determining in their movement.

During the summer I will take a number of ferrets out into the fields on my morning dog walk. When I reach an appropriate spot I will release the ferrets from the well-ventilated pet carrier in which they travel during the hot weather and allow them to explore new and varied locations. My mongrel bitch, Sally, helps me to keep an eye on them and small bells fitted to a ferret collar are another good idea for helping to keep track of their wanderings. Whilst out on such a walk one day, I released two jills for their exercise by a shallow stream and watched curiously as one of them, Scruffy, went down to the water's edge, saw something on the other side that caught her interest and promptly swam very capably and confidently to the other bank. From that time onwards I have offered my ferrets the opportunity to swim provided the weather is warm enough so that they will not become chilled when they get out.

Daily exercise will provide the ferreter with fit and hardy animals and is probably one of the most entertaining chores to be undertaken by the owner. There are various options for providing stimulating exercise reflecting the creativity of the keeper such as artificial warrens, sand pits and an assortment of carefully placed drain pipes, but the main thing is the contentment of the animal with what is offered.

Exercising the ferret in such a way helps to build its confidence, get it used to being handled away from its familiar environment and prepares it for the working season ahead as well as providing interesting stimuli for the animal's senses.

The Importance of a Clean Environment

Despite what many people may think, ferrets are clean animals and appreciate a suitable and hygienic environment in which to live. Most of the visitors to my ferret shed comment on how clean the animals are kept, which is obviously pleasing and in all honesty it does not take that much effort. The importance of maintaining such an environment is to eliminate the risk of disease, foot rot and parasitical lodgers, prevent the build-up of noxious odours, promote the longevity of the cage and provide a hygienic eating and play area.

The process of cage cleaning involves the removal of the litter corner, turning the remaining wood shavings and checking the bedding material after which fresh wood shavings are scattered where required and any new bedding placed within the sleeping compartment. If the wood of the cage's litter corner is stained or particularly damp, it is worth washing it liberally with disinfectant and leaving it exposed to the air to dry before the new material is placed within it.

A variety of materials have and are used for litter including ash, sand, straw, wood bark, shredded paper and sawdust, however, the most popular and best option is a bale of wood shavings. None of the others absorbs as much moisture without producing a sodden smell or is as easy to remove from the cage. Most wood shavings also have a pleasant smell and give a

Although not as proficient as its relative, the semi-aquatic mink, the ferret is a strong and capable swimmer.

I only let my ferrets swim in fresh water and when the weather is warm enough to dry their fur.

fresh appearance to the cage. My brother and I have experimented with other materials especially when a local farmer presented us with a free supply of straw. We used to roll the straw into cylinders of 2–3in in diameter and place them next to one another on the cage floor. Once the end cylinder became well soiled we would remove it and move the next one along whilst placing a new straw cylinder at the opposite end so that a cycle was established. This worked reasonably well, but damp straw produces an unpleasant smell which it transfers onto the ferret.

The most common bedding materials are hay and straw, but shredded paper and wood chips have also been suggested although to my mind the latter two fail to provide the ferret with what it needs to make a comfortable bed. Ferrets love to mould a nest around themselves and in order to do this the material used must be able to maintain a shape, be soft in appearance and have reasonable heat-keeping properties. I have used hay and straw within the sleeping compartments of my ferret cages and both make excellent nests. I only change the bedding material when the nest made by the ferrets begins to collapse, usually once a month, and then I remove it to the run and litter area where it is mixed thoroughly with the wood shavings.

For removal of spent material you cannot better a small hand-held shovel used in conjunction with a home-made or wallpaper scraper. These allow the keeper to take the soiled area with the minimum of wastage. It is

Essential cleaning equipment and replacement material. From left to right: meadow hay for bedding, one bucket for the removal of litter and the other for water, small hand shovel, dustbin bags, scourer, handbrush and dust-extracted wood shavings.

Water is essential for the life, health and comfort of the ferret and should be made constantly available. Water bottles are best because bowls will be upturned.

also worth having a scourer, disinfectant that is not harmful to animals, a good hand brush and three buckets, one for waste, the other for fresh wood shavings and the last one for water.

Wood shavings and hay are available from most equestrian and feed suppliers and are most economically bought as bales. At the moment I am paying £4.50 for a bale of wood shavings which will last approximately two weeks when used to replenish the five large cages in which our twenty ferrets reside. This takes into account the fact that I like to have at least an inch-deep layer of the shavings on the cage floor and will clean the cages on a daily basis. A bale of hay will cost from £3.00 to £5.00 at present and will last me a minimum of two months.

The Importance of Feeding Daily

Before acquiring ferrets it is wise to consider what the animals are to be fed on and where such feed can be procured. If one is obtaining mature animals thought should be given to their existing diet provided by the previous owner.

Animals which have been rescued must also be assessed carefully regarding their dietary needs.

Like most ferreters my brother and I expected a large proportion of the ferrets' food to be provided by our catches; however, our number

The complete diet which I give to my ferrets. The bulk roughage provided by the day-old chicks is complemented with vitamin and mineral-rich ewe's replacement milk.

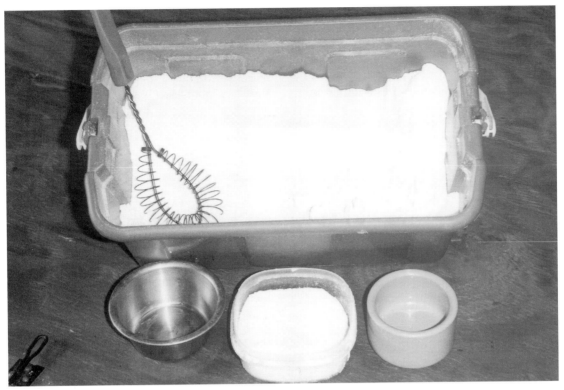

Ewe's replacement milk. This is made into a nourishing drink by mixing 1 part powder with 5–7 parts water and whisking vigorously. It should be served in sturdy bowls.

of ferrets increased faster than our access to quality land and we were faced with a dilemma in what to feed our little army. As most keepers do, our first recourse was to peruse the relevant books and see what they recommended. Our books are a mixture of old and new which meant that one said yes to milk slops and no to meat while the other said yes to flesh and no to milk slops. The easiest lesson is that given by nature which shows the ferret to be a carnivore with a fundamental diet consisting of whole carcasses and water. Therefore, we had to find a supply of meat which was affordable, locally available and appetizing for the ferrets. Our options were processed meat, butchers' offcuts, dry food or whole carcasses.

We tried canned meat to start with which is easy to get hold of and will be eaten by ferrets. However, they soon appeared to tire of it and failed to maintain as good dentition as when fed whole carcass and we noticed that they had a greater susceptibility to abscess formation. Consequently, we moved onto butchers' offcuts consisting mainly of ox hearts and lights which are various parts of the respiratory organs. These kept the ferrets fat, but our wallets thin and at the time we could not sustain such a continual expenditure. It was then that we stumbled across day-old chicks which falconers use to feed their birds and claim to be more nutritious than rabbit. At a price of between three and six pence a day per ferret we were delighted with our find and have fed our ferrets day-olds ever since.

In order to ensure that the diet is not deficient in vitamins and minerals, particularly calcium, we provide our animals with a moderate daily drink of ewe's replacement milk which certainly makes up for any shortcomings that a flesh diet may incur. We use ewe's replacement milk because it comes in powder form and can be made to the consistency required by the user; consequently we have been able to offer it without any detrimental effects to the ferrets. Cow's milk can alternatively be given, but less in quantity and more occasionally. Whilst milk sops should only be given to the ferret as a treat now and again, it is worth knowing how to make a bowlful properly. To prepare bread and milk, use stale bread, pour over it boiling water and compress the bread to expel as much water as possible, then pour over the bread fresh or skimmed milk. Mix up well, add more scalded bread if the food is too liquid and feed while it is lukewarm. An alternative for a treat is Coronation milk diluted with a small amount of hot water and whisked together with egg yolk;

this is particularly good for a ferret that is failing to gain a good weight.

A constant supply of water should be available to the ferret because it is vital to life and health. This is delivered via standard pet water bottles which clip onto the wire front of a cage and are successfully used by ferrets to satisfy their thirst. The best way to keep these bottles clean is to put completely fresh water in every other day.

I have compiled a short list of the most commonly asked questions about feeding a ferret together with brief answers so that it may act as a quick reference.

1. How Much Does It Cost to Feed a Ferret?
This will depend on the diet chosen by the owner. I am currently spending between 3p and 6p per day per ferret using day-old chicks as the staple diet. The relatively new and acclaimed dry food produced by James Wellbeloved claims

Even when feeding the tame ferret can be trusted not to bite.

to cost 10p per day and you certainly do not need to pay more than 10p a day per ferret. Obviously, during the rabbiting season the cost will be reduced.

2. What Type of Food Should I Feed a Ferret?
The staple diet of the ferret should naturally be the fresh meat favoured by the carnivore comprising fur or feather, flesh and bone.

3. How Often Does a Ferret Need Feeding?
The ferret should be fed every day of the week and preferably at the same time. I give my ferrets a drink of replacement milk every morning and their main meal at 4pm. Times are variable according to the wishes of the keeper, but should be as regular as possible.

4. Where Can Suitable Food be Purchased?
Obviously, you can try the local butcher or inquire at the local veterinary surgery. Other sources are direct purchase from James Wellbeloved or if you obtain a copy of *Cage and Aviary Bird*, you will find suppliers of raptor food such as day-old chicks, mice, and so on. Day-olds are sold frozen and the going rate is £30 per 1,000 and some suppliers will deliver to your door if you are willing to pay extra.

5. How Do I Know if I Am Feeding My Ferret the Right Food?
A ferret which is on a correct diet will receive its food with enthusiasm and consume the entire portion offered. It will also be free from ailments, maintain a good weight, display a well-conditioned coat, have bright eyes and sound movement.

6. How Much Food Does a Ferret Need?
This will depend on the size and sex of the animal and the amount of exercise or work that

The food given to the ferret should be palatable and enthusiastically received.

Chewing upon fur and feather enables the ferret to maintain good dentition.

it undertakes. Hobs usually have larger portions than jills. At present my hobs receive two and a half day-olds each per day as their main meat meal.

The subject of ferret food is a contentious issue amongst many ferret keepers and there are a wide variety of different opinions about what constitutes the best diet. My ferrets have been on the same diet for the previous five years and have been free from any ailments during this time. Both young and old alike display vigour and vitality and enjoy the best possible condition – a good standard against which any diet should be measured.

Summary of Needs - The Duties of a Ferret Keeper

1 Release ferrets from their cages for free exercise under supervision or within an ark. Observe animals' movement and alertness.

2 Clean out litter corner and any damp wood shavings from the cage. Replenish with fresh wood shavings. Check bedding material and nest for any buried food.

3 Return ferrets to their cages with a drink of replacement milk. Wash milk bowls.

4 Feed day-olds to ferrets. Ensure that each animal is getting its fair share and eating normally, that is, with appetite and good chewing action. Check water bottles and cage locks.

5 Some time each day should be spent handling the ferrets and checking their health.

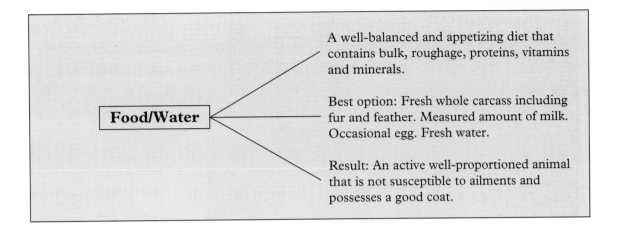

	A well-balanced and appetizing diet that contains bulk, roughage, proteins, vitamins and minerals.
Food/Water	Best option: Fresh whole carcass including fur and feather. Measured amount of milk. Occasional egg. Fresh water.
	Result: An active well-proportioned animal that is not susceptible to ailments and possesses a good coat.

A Place Called Home

Adequate accommodation is a fundamental need and moral right of a domesticated animal and significant for the ferreter because of the amount of time that the ferret will spend in the cage, the contributory effect it makes to the health and welfare of the animal and plainly because the ferret cannot be kept without providing a proper home for it.

With the welcome news that a ferret had finally been located and would be arriving the following week, my brother raided my father's wood supply and waltzed off with any half decent off-cuts he could find. There followed the resonant chorus of the hammer falling upon nail after nail and the wood ripping unwillingly as the saw was ham-fistedly driven through it until my brother finally emerged with a cage that could best be described as rough and ready. Many ferreters begin in exactly the same fashion by making a cage out of what materials are readily to hand and there is nothing wrong with this approach providing that the cage is secure, well-ventilated and has an enclosed sleeping compartment and separate litter corner. I have

This converted duck shed provides the ferrets with their essential housing requirements, that is, warmth, space and ventilation.

Commercial cages are intended for rabbits and should be made ferret-proof by replacing the wire with stout aviary wire, of maximum mesh size 25 x 13mm. A board incorporated in the door to prevent wood shavings being wasted is a useful modification.

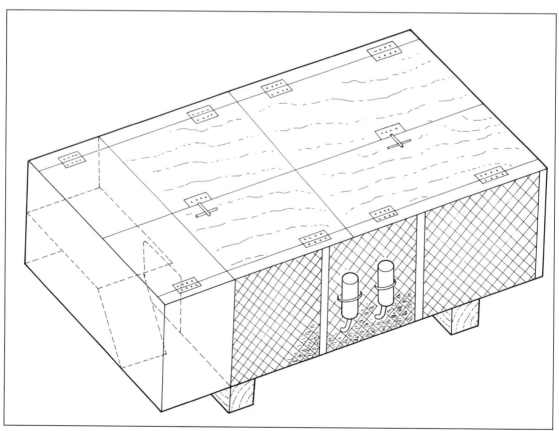

An 8ft x 4ft (2.5m x 1.25m) inside cage which I built to house eight ferrets. Split lids allow me access to every corner and wire on all sides provides the ferrets with plenty of light. The cage is held together by screws and corner brackets so that it can be completely dismantled for an overhaul once a year.

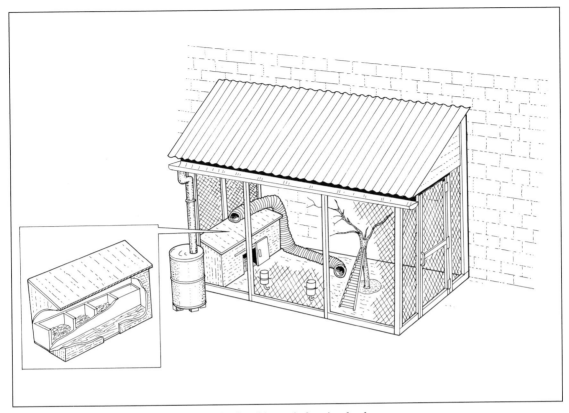

A typical ferret court considered by many to be the ultimate in housing for the ferret. Note the integral sleeping box and drainage system.

made satisfactory cages from odds and ends such as antiquated wine crates and reclaimed barn flooring from a local farm.

At the other end of the scale, I have bought commercially made, expensive cages that need minor adaptations to make them ferret proof. The wire is rarely strong enough gauge and there is no sawdust catching board, but, these are easily added. The benefits of a bought cage are its ease of acquisition, tidy appearance, strong construction and longetivity owing to the fact that it is made of new materials. If you do not fancy building your own cage or converting an existing structure and money is not at a premium, then buying a ready-made cage is the best option.

Most of the ferreters whom I have known make their own cages with their preferences

borne in mind and I must confess that my DIY skills have improved no end since I began to keep ferrets. Home-made cages can be made to various sizes and designs and are good value for money with the economy increasing as the proportions of the cage get bigger. They will also be made particularly with ferrets in mind and incorporate special features. However, making your own cage is a time-consuming endeavour and does require some dexterity.

When my brother and I became tired of attending to our ferrets in inclement weather conditions we moved them into a 6ft x 4ft shed in which were placed some sleeping boxes. These enabled us to handle and clean the ferrets for as long as we wanted irrespective of the weather and gave the ferrets a much larger and more interesting environment in which to exercise. As well as being the ferrets' home, the shed provided a place for storing all our rabbiting equipment and attending to such routine tasks as claw clipping and ear cleaning. Small sheds start at about £100 and therefore to house ferrets in a shed requires a reasonable initial expenditure; however, with the increase in price of cages, I believe the shed to be better value for money.

Many of the traditional ferreters who had large numbers of animals used to keep them in what is termed a ferret court which is practically a miniature stockyard with boxes. The floor should be slightly sloping and made of hard material and a set of sleeping boxes arranged at the top end of the court where they are sheltered and draught proof. The whole structure should be enclosed within wire and a door provided for access of the keeper. Such structures have a secure environment in which the ferret can exercise when it wishes, but they are expensive to make and very difficult to move.

The type of housing that a keeper will select will depend upon how many ferrets are owned and whether they get on with one another. Another choice is whether to keep the cages inside or outside and this will depend upon preference because both options are acceptable. I favour keeping my ferret cages within outbuild-ings or sheds because they are protected from the worst of the weather during both summer and winter and a shed incorporates a convenient exercise area. Furthermore, it provides a haven in which the ferreter can leisurely take stock of his animals in peace and quiet.

Acquisition

'Ferrets are what we need' my brother declared as we examined the damage caused by rats to the underside of our recently restored chicken shed. Consequently, the search for a ferret began and our exasperated parents were sent to and fro, up and down the green byways and country lanes from one eccentric character to another who used to keep ferrets and probably knew somebody who continued to do so. Their inquiries terminated at the doorstep of a local gamekeeper who knew of a youngster who had grown weary of his two albinos and was looking to rehome them. We discovered that ferrets are not as easy to obtain as they used to be when every village had at least one person who kept and worked ferrets. However, there are a number of options for the person who wishes to keep a ferret or the established keeper who wants to increase his stock.

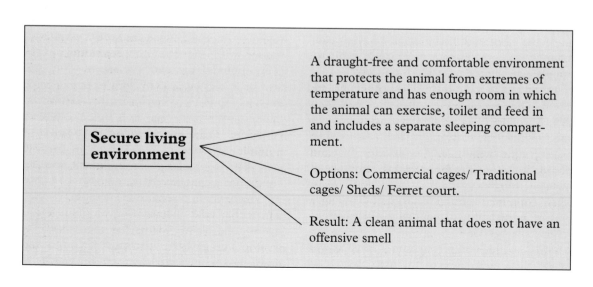

Secure living environment

A draught-free and comfortable environment that protects the animal from extremes of temperature and has enough room in which the animal can exercise, toilet and feed in and includes a separate sleeping compart-ment.

Options: Commercial cages/ Traditional cages/ Sheds/ Ferret court.

Result: A clean animal that does not have an offensive smell

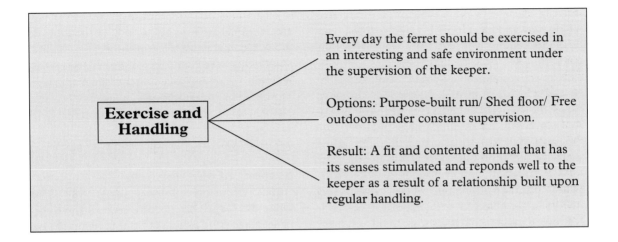

Every day the ferret should be exercised in an interesting and safe environment under the supervision of the keeper.

Options: Purpose-built run/ Shed floor/ Free outdoors under constant supervision.

Result: A fit and contented animal that has its senses stimulated and reponds well to the keeper as a result of a relationship built upon regular handling.

Exercise and Handling

The most obvious way to obtain a ferret is to purchase one and the old advice of buying from a reputable breeder is still relevant. You will be likely to find these advertised in the local press, at your vet's or in the *Countryman's Weekly*. On the rare occasions when I have purchased ferrets, I have endeavoured to locate a breeder who works his animals, either for sport or pest control, and therefore keeps them fit and well handled. The fun of purchasing ferrets is in choosing how many, and of what sex, physique and colour. The ferret will also have been initially tamed and will have matured past the age where kit mortality is a danger. The usual age at which a ferret is bought is between two and three months, although some breeders may offer a tame and proven worker for a higher price which is worth considering for the person who has access to land heavily populated with rabbits. The disadvantages lie in the time and expense of locating and then buying from a good source. However, it is always interesting to meet people who have enthusiasm for and knowledge about the ferret and the expense of travel or purchase is a very small investment when compared with the benefit of having a healthy animal of one's own choosing.

The second way to obtain a ferret is to rehome or rescue one. The rehoming of ferrets is primarily concerned with finding con-scientious owners for animals which have been restored to full fitness after having previously been lost or neglected in some fashion. Many leading welfare organizations have at some time or other ferrets available for rehoming and the animals will be well handled and require a clean bill of health before being offered to a new owner who must prove his suitability for having a ferret. If a person already has a knowledge of ferrets he may wish to rescue them directly by operating a service within his local area. Before contemplating rescuing ferrets, one must first possess the self-assurance to be able to deal with a ferret effectively, irrespective of its state of mind or health. Secondly, the amount of time that a sick, recovering or aggressive animal will require means that the keeper must place working with, and for, ferrets as a major priority in the cycle of daily life. It is always satisfying to be involved in the restoration of the rescued or rehomed ferret to health and happiness. There are, however, disadvantages in that it cannot be predicted when a ferret will be available and the age of the animal is usually a matter of guesswork. Most rehoming centres will also want to spay or castrate the animal before they will release it from their care. Happily, the ability of the ferret to work and develop a relationship with the keeper are not diminished by its negative experiences or more mature age and some of the most interesting characters and most reliable workers that I have encountered have found their way to me via such routes.

For the established keeper who wishes to increase his stock there is the obvious choice of breeding his own animals or forming a co-operative with fellow sportsmen. In either case he must make careful selection of the breeding animals and thorough preparation for the care of a pregnant jill and eventually newborn kits. The advantage of breeding is that of choosing the animals involved with the hope of replicating certain characteristics and thereby establish a breeding line. The enthusiastic owner also gains satisfaction from successful breeding and is able to determine the health, welfare and growing environment from day one. On the negative side, numbers cannot be predicted and neither can gender.

Clearly, there are no shortages of ferrets available for ownership and a circumspect appraisal of the different situations of availability will enable one to select a course of action that suits one best.

Systems of Management

Once the keeper has acquired a healthy supply of animals, he is faced with the decision of how best to keep them. The options are to keep the animals separately, in small groups or in a commune. During my years of ferret-keeping,

---

The Ferret's Living Environment.

(a) Why is it important?

1. The length of time the ferret will spend in the cage.
2. Contribution to health and welfare of the animal.
3. The ferret cannot be kept without providing housing for it.

(b) What characteristics should it possess?

1. It should be secure.
2. It should be well ventilated and have an enclosed compartment for sleeping.
3. It should have provision of a litter corner at the farthest distance from the sleeping box.

(c) What should it provide the ferret with?

1. Space.
2. Shelter.
3. Stimulation.

(d) How should it be constructed to make life easier for the keeper?

1. Avoid joins on the inside. All battens on exterior of structure.
2. Make all corners of the cage easily accessible.
3. Treat timber before using it.
4. Include a sawdust catching board.

(e) What materials should be used and what size should the cage be?

1. A quarter to half-inch thick exterior plywood.
2. Tanalized tongue and groove.
3. Welded mesh wire.
4. Roofing felt or onduline for exterior cages.
5. Door hinges, clasp and lock.

I have practised all three systems of management and realized that each has its respective pros and cons.

Separate Management

Should a single ferret be caged, exercised, worked and fed on its own? I have heard it said that no less than two ferrets should be kept together on the hypothesis that a single animal will suffer from loneliness and be deprived of the opportunity to play. Does this therefore infer that a person who only wants to keep one ferret should think again and either not bother with any ferrets at all or buy a minimum of two animals? The lesson of nature appears to suggest not, because the European polecat, commonly believed to be the ancestor of the ferret, like most mustelids is a territorial animal that lives a solitary life except for during the breeding season. This would lead one to the conclusion that the influence of man on the development and management of the ferret is the only reason for its co-habitation.

I have kept ferrets singly and have encountered ferret enthusiasts who have only possessed the one animal and in all cases without exception the ferret has not suffered any deficiency through lack of company of its own species. However, all such keepers were prepared to spend a substantial amount of time exercising, playing with and handling the single animal. In my experience a ferret by itself that is the recipient of such attention develops a greater affinity with the keeper in a shorter amount of time and arguably becomes tamer more quickly.

Some of the advantages to only managing a single animal are as follows:

1. It costs less which is of particular importance to the growing ranks of young children who keep ferrets.
2. It is easier to free exercise a single ferret because one's concentration is not divided.
3. A ferret which does not have other animals of its own kind to play with will often try to encourage play with the owner.

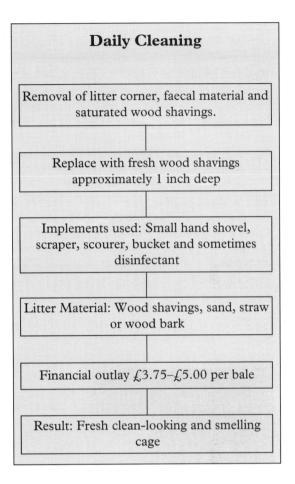

Daily Cleaning

Removal of litter corner, faecal material and saturated wood shavings.

Replace with fresh wood shavings approximately 1 inch deep

Implements used: Small hand shovel, scraper, scourer, bucket and sometimes disinfectant

Litter Material: Wood shavings, sand, straw or wood bark

Financial outlay £3.75–£5.00 per bale

Result: Fresh clean-looking and smelling cage

4. It is easier to give one animal rather than a number of them the attention and time that they should be given.

The disadvantages of only having one ferret are:

1. Its limitations for working. Most ardent ferreters agree that to work seriously they require a minimum stock of two ferrets.
2. The ferret will require more from the keeper because it does not have playmates to tire it.

Although I would suggest that an ideal number for the person who wants to work ferrets traditionally is between two and six, the fact remains that if you only want to keep one ferret, there is no reason why you should not. To argue that a ferret needs the company of other ferrets has little validity and is akin to suggesting that a dog should not be kept singly, but in a pack formation in order to be happy. It is not a matter of numbers that will determine the well-being of the animal, but giving it the correct amount of care and attention and it certainly does not amount to cruelty to keep just one ferret.

Group Management

If the keeper starts with one ferret there is nothing to stop him adding to his stock at a later date and a ferret that has been used to living by itself will integrate with new company. Group living differs from the traditional commune system in that it comprises a number of animals, no less than three and no more than six, living in suitably sized cages rather than a large complex in which all the animals intermingle.

When my brother and I had an unexpected influx of rescue cases some years ago we had little option but to accommodate them in groups. If the ferret keeper has a number of animals and chooses to house them in groups, all newcomers will need to be introduced to existing stock and entire ferrets reintegrated with their cohort when the breeding season is complete. The establishment of groups entails a mix of age, gender and character and necessitates careful thought regarding the best time and candidates for integration.

Keeping ferrets in groups brings benefits for both the handler and his creatures when they are

Ferrets enjoy the close company of their own species and willingly nest together.

working in the field and during daily management. These include:

1. Savings for the pocket, as less litter and cages are required; of energy, as there are fewer cages to clean, and of time, as a large group of creatures can be handled concurrently rather than one after another.
2. Group living provides the gregarious ferret with the company of its own species at all times, facilitates play and exercise and establishes the basis for successful corporate working endeavours on intensive warren systems.

In opposition to group living it has been suggested that:

1. A ferret that lives with members of its own species is apt to bond to those members in preference to its keeper.
2. The animals compete for food and must be carefully watched to ensure an equity of distribution.
3. There are reasons for continued segregation which are the preference of the owner for single-system management, the keeping of a traditional line ferret and the clear manifestation of unhappy behaviour experienced either by the individual or the group with which it is integrating. Temporary isolation is essential during the breeding season and when an animal is sick and requires nursing attention.

Groups may be established by either keeping a number of littermates or introducing ferrets of different breeding and ages to one another. Although ferrets are individuals and respond in their own time and manner to new company, the resolute oversight of the handler will contribute to reducing the stress of meeting. Firstly, one must ensure that the newcomer is ready in terms of health, fitness, maturity and tameness to meet with other ferrets and this is especially vital if a ferret has been rescued or rehomed from an animal sanctuary in which

case all ailments must be treated and operations recovered from. If a batch of kits are to be introduced to senior ferrets, they must have reached a stage of development that enables them to assert themselves and not be overwhelmed by the physique of older animals. Obviously, entire animals should not be introduced until the completion of the breeding season due to their ability to procreate and the manifestation of aggressive behaviour arising from the mating impulse. Ferrets that are fit and well can be introduced on an uncluttered shed floor with which they are both familiar during their normal daily exercise time. Such an environment provides the ferrets with security, freedom of movement and space to escape unwanted attention and enables the handler to make timely interventions if required. It is not advisable to introduce ferrets that are cage-bound, or at mealtimes, because the animals will understandably be at their most defensive and fiercely competitive.

If all goes well at this stage, and it usually does, the ferrets can be placed together in an exercise run. The exercise run provides a more confined environment in which the ferrets can be left for prolonged periods of time. A greater variety of behaviour is experienced, including play and sleep, as the time away from the cage is extended and the habit of the ferrets to curl up together is evidence of their bonding and prepares them for sharing the nest. This process may be repeated daily for as long as is necessary for familiarity to be established. The final stage of integration is to place the animals in a suitably sized cage where they will learn to feed together.

The path of integrating ferrets does not always run smoothly and there are signs to watch out for that all is not well. Among these are odorous release from the scent glands, a fanned tail, continual high-pitched squealing and constant running away from the advancing ferret. Although some noise and wrestling are to be expected when introducing ferrets, this should not be of a prolonged nature or cause excessive stress. If any of these behaviours become apparent the hapless victim should be rescued from his torment and placed in a separate cage where he can receive his needs in a stress-free environment. There are some ferrets that do not respond well to the company of their own species, either because of the way in which they have been reared or due to a distressing incident arising from a badly managed introduction, and for animals such as these a separated life is clearly a happier one.

Commune Management

A commune or court system of ferret management was considered earlier this century to be the ideal way to keep the animals in a happy and healthy fashion. A commune system is as its name suggests the co-habitation of a large number of ferrets of both sexes, various ages and different bloodlines. Courts are good for keepers whose work does not allow much time for seeing and exercising the ferrets every day during the week and have an area large enough to incorporate multiple litter corners which may need cleaning out only once or twice a week. The court gives the ferret the optimum amount of enclosed space and pro-

vides them with the largest secure area for free movement.

A court system requires an enormous amount of allotted room and space and careful thought must be given to the design so that it is draught-free, leak-proof and one hundred per cent secure. As such the materials for construction are quite costly and a court will be time-consuming to build. In terms of actual management of the animals, it may prove difficult to introduce new stock to an established group. Jills and entire hobs will need separating during the breeding season to prevent the occurrence of multiple litters. The ferrets should be closely observed for any signs and symptoms of malady so that sick and ailing animals can be isolated in order to prevent the possible spread of any infection and provide the sick animal with the individualized care it requires. It is not worth considering the option of a commune unless the keeper has a minimum of ten ferrets which can live happily together throughout the four seasons of the year. In my experience the best commune population consists of hoblets and jills.

4 MANAGEMENT OF THE SICK ANIMAL

Off Colour

I have found the ferret to be a robust and hardy animal which when kept in proper conditions enjoys good health and is surprisingly free from serious ailments. However, for any keeper of animals there is the possibility that at some time he will encounter the occurrence of disease, sickness or injury amongst his stock and for this reason he must be able to recognize and interpret the earliest manifestation of symptoms. The rapid onset of illness is an unfortunate feature of the ferret which can appear to be able to take on the world one day and be at death's door the next. On the other side of the coin, the recovery of an ailing ferret can be just as dramatic with revitalization seeming to take hardly any time at all and being accomplished with the minimum of fuss.

One of the most influential factors determining the outcome of any ailment is prompt treatment which is only initiated by those who conduct routine observation of their animals. The best practice of a keeper is to spend a couple of minutes each day handling and watching each ferret in his possession whilst mentally rehearsing a simple checklist designed to clearly identify the animal's state of well-being. Such a checklist should take account of the appetite, appearance, movement and behaviour of the ferret and take note of any deviation away from normal functioning and routine.

Early recognition of something being wrong derived from this careful approach enables the keeper to assess the need to isolate and monitor the ferret more closely, initiate veterinary intervention and the administration of medication and provide for any special needs the animal may have.

The experienced keeper who knows his animals well will have developed a sixth sense for noticing when they are off colour and will be familiar with the most commonly occurring and apparent symptoms which are:

1. General malaise and tiredness.
2. Failure to rise.
3. Slow or unsteady movement.
4. Loss of appetite.
5. Laboured breathing.
6. Fluid secretions from eyes and nose.
7. Hair loss.
8. Lump formation that can be felt.
9. Abnormal elimination.
10. Any unexplained variation in normal behaviour.

With the appearance of any of these symptoms further investigation is recommended either by the keeper who has experienced morbidity in ferrets previously or by a veterinarian, following which an appropriate course of action can be decided upon.

Routine Health Care

The keeper must be prepared to maintain his animals in the best possible condition and will therefore need to attend regularly to chores which if left undone would result in neglect. Each of the activities listed below is easy to perform, does not require much time and undeniably benefits the ferret.

Claw Clipping

The ferret has a non-retractile claw proceeding from each of its five toes on both front and back legs. Some maintain that these claws do not need trimming based on the premise that exercise will, by wear and tear, manage the claws at a naturally comfortable length for the ferret. However, I have not found this to be the case amongst my animals which are exercised on hard and soft surfaces daily and even lost ferrets that I have rescued from feral living need their claws clipping as a matter of urgency. Admittedly, if a ferrets claws are allowed to grow unchecked they may reach a stage where the excess will break off, but this brings with it the possibility of a split or painful claw. Also to reach this stage the claws will be copiously overgrown and liable to adversely affect the comfort of walking.

Ferret claws may be clipped with nail scissors or conventional dog claw cutters. The claws should be clipped one after another and trimmed back so that they are equal with either the base of the pad or the ball of each respective toe. The ferret should be held securely throughout the operation to avoid the risk of slipping and cutting the quick which contains blood vessels and is sensitive to pain. The claws are a commonly used tool of the ferret and care should be taken to make sure that they are cut to the right length. I have found that the claws of the front feet need more regular trimming than those of the back, and that on average the former should be cut every month and the latter every three months.

Whether it be a dog, cat or ferret, owners seem most nervous about cutting through the quick of the nail. If this does happen there will be a continuous small discharge of blood and a very unhappy animal. A moist bar of soap, some

The ferret medicine chest with sufficient contents to enable me to deal with routine tasks, common ailments and minor injuries.

candle wax or Vaseline should be gently rubbed across the end of the nail to stem the bleeding and the animal should be held still for a couple of moments to recover from the shock. Fortunately, the pain quickly subsides and the animal is very forgiving to its keeper. My ferrets are tame and are held easily in one hand while I clip their nails and therefore should they suddenly start to struggle or move their head in a startled fashion, I always relax the pressure on the clippers and recheck the position and by so listening to my animals prevent making mistakes and causing them pain. Clearly, there is no reason why a ferret should have to endure the discomfort of overgrown nails.

Ear Cleansing

Oddly, I have some ferrets whose ears remain spotlessly clean and others who harbour waxy deposits in the hairy folds of their ear flaps. The ear flaps which are obviously visible as projections on either side of the ferret's head should be cleaned gently with a cotton wool bud and a separate bud should be used for each ear flap. The ear proper or internal ear should on no account be poked and prodded to remove waxy deposits, no matter how delicate the probe may appear because such endeavours may well damage sensitive membrane and impair the function of hearing. It is much better practice to insert ear drops on a regular basis as they will soften the wax and enable the dissolution and free drainage of any build-up of wax. Before giving ear drops, the dispenser should be carried in a pocket and then rubbed up and down between the hands to warm the fluid that will then be more penetrating and soothing. As an alternative to ear drops a small amount of olive or sunflower oil may be used.

If the keeper suspects that there is a serious blockage in the ear, he should consult the vet who has the skill necessary to employ more invasive procedures to rectify the situation. When cleaning a ferret's ears, it is a good idea to hold the animal over a bale of hay so that, if it twists free as they sometimes do, it will not fall onto a hard surface such as a concrete floor.

Eye Cleaning

On rare occasions my ferrets have emerged with one eye fastened shut in comical fashion which has been due to the presence of a foreign body such as large grains of dust, seeds or grit. If the keeper finds himself faced with such a problem he should hold the eyelids gently apart and if the offending article can be seen, remove it with the corner of some newly opened gauze. If the keeper cannot see the cause of complaint it is worth performing an eye wash with some Optrex or saline. Once again gauze may be used, beginning at the inside of the eye and wiping outwards over the lens. The gauze should be discarded after each movement across the eye. Consequently, the eyes should be inspected on a daily basis and cleaned in the manner mentioned as often as is required.

Grooming

I rarely bother to groom the coats of any of my ferrets, but will make an exception if it gets soiled or mucky whilst playing or working. I have a comb with close metal teeth which is good for knots due to dry mud or less pleasant substances. I do shampoo my ferrets during the summer to aid in the removal of old hair and offer limited protection against parasites as well as to improve the condition of the coat and underlying skin. When shampooing during the summer, I wait until the gentle rays of the sun's heat are cascading down and then place a makeshift table in a warm position. I will then place two buckets of tepid water, shampoo and a towel on the table ready for use. My ferrets are quite at home in the water and will tolerate being dunked before a generous amount of shampoo is well massaged into the coat, taking care to avoid the sensory organs. They are then rinsed off in the second bucket, given a good wipe with a towel and then put in a hay bed where they can complete the drying process themselves. A well-conditioned coat is not only better for the ferret, but makes the creature more of a pleasure to handle.

Health Problems

Thankfully, during my years as a ferret keeper, I have encountered very few serious health problems amongst my animals and have rarely had to consult a vet. Ferret mortalities have most often been due to old age and only on one occasion was I obliged to have a ferret put down due to a paralyzing back injury. Many of the conditions mentioned in this section very rarely affect the ferret and are mentioned merely as reference and a basis for further study should the keeper so desire.

Abscesses

The most common malady that I have witnessed in ferrets is abscess formation situ-

Whether treating abscesses on the neck or parasites around the ears, care should be taken to avoid damaging the ferret's sensory organs.

ated in the neck, lower jaw or cheek. Abscesses appear as large swellings which are hard at first, but become softer as they develop to the point where they are going to burst. They can be accompanied by a fever and may be caused by a puncture wound, the presence of a foreign body, infection or poor diet. Fundamentally, an abscess is a containment of the dead cells, fluid and bacteria, which are collectively known as pus, and enclosed within a wall of lymph. The pus may be healthy in which case it will be yellowish white in colour, free from offensive odour and possessing the consistency of cream and can be reabsorbed into the ferret's system harmlessly. Alternatively, unhealthy pus could be present which is characterized by an offensive smell and can contain blood, mucus or a thin and watery substance that, when reabsorbed, results in the condition known as toxaemia.

Thanks to years of successful treatment of abscesses documented prior to the widespread use of antibiotics, the keeper may effectively treat his animal if he is absolutely certain of what he is dealing with. The old-fashioned or traditional method for dealing with an abscess is to apply a home-made poultice and there was a time when every stockman was adept at making a poultice with herbal ingredients according to a recipe handed down from generation to generation. Herbalists and physicians in years gone by commonly used the application of a poultice to the skin to draw pus or foreign bodies from a wound. A poultice is essentially a pack containing fresh or dried herbs, boiling water and bread which maintains the heat and should be as hot as the patient can comfortably bear it. Traditional herbs used in the formation of a poultice to treat an abscess include garlic, sage, marjoram and oregano. The poultice once made can be used time and again providing that it is reheated and not contaminated with blood or pus. When pressed against an abscess on a ferret in all practicality it is only feasible to hold it in place for a matter of minutes at any one given time; however, allowing for rest, this

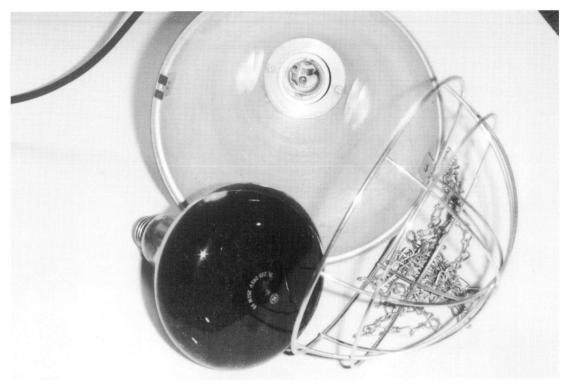

A broody lamp commonly used for maintaining vital heat for chicks can also be used to good effect when a ferret is sick and its thermoregulatory system compromised.

process can be repeated as many as four to six times a day.

Should the abscess burst either of its own accord or as the result of some gentle squeezing all the pus should be drained before a poultice is reapplied. If the rupture of the abscess has left an open wound a liberal amount of honey can be spread over it to promote healing. My brother first used honey on a hobbling cat he encountered that had through injury lost part of two toes on one of its hind paws. He had previously watched a programme on the remarkable healing properties of honey and decided to have a go himself. The vet he consulted agreed that the treatment would prove effective and of course cost a lot less than conventional antibiotics. He gave my brother an iodine solution with which to wash the affected paw and wished him luck. Although

the cat trusted my brother, it was not easy to handle the paw for treatment because of the pain that it caused. After my brother had managed to bathe and dry the squirming paw, he applied a liberal amount of honey and a non-stick dressing which he managed to secure in place with surgical tape. The wound was redressed on a daily basis and the dressings he removed were thick and sticky with an odorous tar-like substance that continued to be produced by the wound for the period of one week. After a fortnight the terrible injury was healed with the scar tissue taking on a nice pink colour that suitably impressed the vet. Consequently, if you are faced with an open wound on the body of one of your ferrets as the result of an abscess or injury reach for a jar of honey.

My brother and I have successfully treated a number of abscesses in the above-mentioned manner, but if you are of a more conventional disposition the vet will be able to lance the abscess and start your animal on a course of antibiotics. I have injected my ferrets with antibiotics prescribed by the vet and witnessed good results, but much prefer the more natural method because I feel it causes less stress for the animal.

If the ferret-keeper has repeated incidence of abscess formation amongst his stock he should reassess their diet, making sure that there is sufficient fur, feather and cartilage to promote teeth cleaning.

Alopecia

Hair loss in the ferret may be caused by mange, poor diet or hormonal imbalance. They will exhibit some hair loss characteristically at the beginning and end of the breeding season but this should quickly remedy itself. Sometimes a hob which has undergone surgery for castration will have a thinning of the coat, This is not unusual and can be rectified with an injection administered by the vet.

One of my most active white jills called Scruffy went through a period of drastic hair loss of unknown cause when she was younger. Apart from her head and neck she was more or less without a coat to speak of and could not maintain her usual body heat. Therefore, I provided her with a warm environment, increased her diet and lessened her exercise until her condition improved. I also rubbed a neutral gel into her skin to prevent it becoming dry and irritable. My brother attempted to make her a little jacket from an old sweat shirt, but Scruffy cast it aside with disdain as anything that impedes a ferret's movements is resented and likely to end up in the corner of the cage.

Botulism

This is a severe form of food poisoning produced by the bacterium *Clostridium Botulinum* which leaves its spores in decaying animal or plant matter where they multiply and manufacture a very lethal toxin. There is no treatment and therefore the utmost attention should be given to providing the ferrets always with fresh meat. Should a ferret exhibit difficulty eating, show a gross lack of co-ordination and slight paralysis it must be taken to the vet at the earliest opportunity. If his diagnosis is botulism, have the animal put down without delay.

Colds

It is now believed that ferrets catch the same strains of cold that affect human beings and so cross-infection is a commonly occurring possibility. If my brother and I catch a cold we keep our distance from the ferret shed as a precaution and wait until we are well rid of the malady before handling the ferrets as usual. The symptoms of a ferret cold do not differ from those found in man and are a wet runny nose, reduced appetite and general loss of vitality. As with us, the ferret will enjoy some pampering and this can include some warm bowls of milk, beef tea and the gentle heat rays of a broody lamp which should soon see the

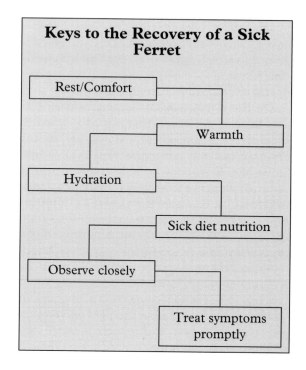

Keys to the Recovery of a Sick Ferret

- Rest/Comfort
- Warmth
- Hydration
- Sick diet nutrition
- Observe closely
- Treat symptoms promptly

animal back to its old self. If recovery is delayed and the ferret's breathing becomes more laboured it should commence a course of antibiotics as prescribed by your vet.

Ferrets will succumb to colds if they are kept in damp and exposed conditions from which they cannot find respite. Therefore, they should be kept in draught-free and waterproof housing and have plenty of bedding material. If the cages are left out in all weathers it is well worth making a protective front out of perspex with which to cover the wire.

Distemper

Distemper is a savage disease that has in the past mercilessly obliterated the entire stock of even the most knowledgeable of ferret-keepers. A lot of contemporary books do not bother mentioning distemper because a successful vaccination has made the disease a rarity. However, this does not mean that the disease has disappeared or is not a threat to ferrets which have not been vaccinated. The distemper that affects ferrets is the same as that which affected the canine world with such ferocity that it become known as the 'dog plague' synonymous with the black death. The control of the disease was only brought about in the 1920s when a fund was established by *The Field* magazine with the specific intention of researching the cause and treatment of the disease.

The first recognizable symptoms of distemper are loss of vitality accompanied by poor appetite, inflammation of the cheeks and gums, dry nose and eyes which are photophobic and have a glutinous appearance. If there is to be any hope of recovery for an animal suffering from the disease it is imperative that an early diagnosis is made and prompt treatment initiated. If the symptoms deteriorate into copious secretions from nose and eyes, shivering, coughing, sneezing, vomiting and enteritis all hopes of recovery have disappeared.

Whilst researching distemper, I discovered that my collection of old manuals claim to have seen animals recover from the virus while the modern works claim that it is incurable. Either these knowledgeable old ferret keepers misdiagnosed the condition and cured the ferrets of some other form of fever or recognized it so quickly and acted with such swiftness that the ferret was able to maintain its condition and empowered to fight the disease. I do not know whether the old ferreters were onto something or not, but it has got to be worth taking their advice and giving the ferret every possible chance. Without doubt the ferret's prospects of surviving are directly linked to the quality of nursing it receives. A ferret which is kept warm under a broody lamp, that is regularly cleansed of any discharges and fed on beef tea is bound to stand a better chance than a weak, cold and hungry animal which will soon succumb to any disease.

To alleviate your concerns regarding your animals contracting distemper you can have them vaccinated at approximately ten weeks of age. A vaccine originating from ferret tissue should not be used as this will give the animal distemper.

Ear mites

Ear mites cause the ferret a great deal of irritation, interfere with its co-ordination and may result in death if left untreated and allowed to permeate the inner ear. A ferret with ear mites will scratch madly at its ears and shake its head violently in an attempt to rid itself of the unwelcome parasite. The ear mite will cause inflammation of the ear and a granular brown deposit will testify to its presence. If you are quick to notice the mite you can administer drops intended for cats which are available in pet shops and should kill the parasite. However, should you have any uncertainty about what to do, how long the mites have been in residence or how badly the animal is affected take it to the vet without delay before the condition worsens.

Fleas

When Mouse, an inoffensive small albino hob, emerged from his daily spell in an exercise run, my brother quickly affirmed that the army of black marching through the ferret's coat was an army of fleas. As he reached for the flea comb in an attempt to quell the tide of this parasitical invasion, a subsequent inspection of our remaining nineteen ferrets revealed that we had unwittingly succumbed to a considerable infestation. Our customary Monday morning routine was abandoned and rearranged to encompass the treatment of animals, cleansing of cages and extermination of fleas. We favour an immediate response because of the discomfort experienced by the ferrets, the rapidity with which the fleas spread among livestock and the knock-on effect on daily handling. Although it has been suggested that the flea can complete its life-cycle on the ferret without being detrimental to the health of the host animal, I would sooner not give them the chance believing that the ferret's general well-being is compromised by the nuisance value of the parasite, the excessive scratching that they excite and the potential for infection that can arise from skin abrasions caused by such scratching.

Consequently, my brother set off for the local town to purchase an array of flea-combating products and replacement bedding material. There are a multitude of proprietary products available, ranging from sprays and powders to shampoos, all of which promise to kill the flea with one application and some of which claim to protect against further infestation for a limited period of time. We favour shampoo if the weather is fine because of the increased control of application, which is vital when treating a small hyperactive animal, and the added benefit of conditioning the coat which is apparent to touch and in appearance. However, if the weather is cooler we tend to opt for a spray, taking care to avoid the eyes, nose and mouth of the ferret.

On this occasion we used shampoo and once

Although not as versatile as the semi-arboreal marten, the ferret is a competent climber.

My ferrets enjoy climbing artificial and natural obstacles and are watched carefully in order to prevent a fall and the possibility of back injury.

we had dried our victims turned our attention to decontaminating their homes and thereby preventing a cycle of parasitical reinfestation. Due to the flea's propensity for evasive egg-laying all bedding and litter material should be removed and an insecticidal spray used to permeate every nook and cranny. Thought should be given to identifying the source from which the infestation sprang and at the time we were understandably bemused because our ferrets, unlike flea-infested ones that we had previously rescued from the wild, had not been in contact with quarry playing host to the parasite. Following a literature search conducted at the local library I came up with a plausible answer based upon the third of the four stages of development that occur during the life of a flea. This is known as the pupal stage where a cocoon has been spun by the larva of the preceding stage and from which the adult flea will emerge. The ability of the flea to remain dormant for up to a year in a cocoon means that it need only emerge when conditions are favourable. My brother and I believe that the use of old hay retrieved from the farmer's barn introduced cocoons into the nesting boxes from which the adult fleas came forth from their dormant state.

It would be a brave person who claimed that his system of livestock management could prevent the occurrence of parasitical invasion, but the simple precautions of maintaining clean cages and only using fresh bedding and litter material will help to lessen the risk or severity of attack. Fortunately, prompt treatment is easy and effective.

Foot rot

Foot rot is essentially a problem related to poor or ill-informed husbandry and is therefore totally avoidable. It produces swollen and scabby feet which are quite painful and if allowed to continue unabated the rot will expose the bone. Damp conditions perpetuated by inadequate litter material and infrequent cleaning of the cage encourage the growth of the fungus which is responsible for foot rot. I have only ever seen one case which was very superficial and hastily remedied by an improved environment.

I keep my ferrets on a thick layer of wood shavings which are replenished on a daily basis. Cage size is also important in preventing damp living conditions underfoot and each ferret should have ample space in which to play and feed well removed from the litter corner. Another controversial practice of some ferreters of yesteryear was to use wire as the floor for a

ferret cage and allow the soiled litter to be trodden through the mesh. I have only ever come across one contemporary keeper who employs this detrimental method of management which does little to prevent the onset of foot rot.

I am in the habit of checking my ferrets' feet every time I handle them and make sure that they are a normal pink colour, clean and free from noxious smells. If the feet failed to comply with any of these requirements, I would have to reassess my cage-cleaning regime and look to improve the hygiene of the ferrets' living quarters. Treatment of foot rot is relatively simple and basically consists of keeping the cage and feet of the ferret clean. The cage should be disinfected in order to destroy the elusive fungal spores that hide in every crevice and the ferrets'

A long back enables the ferret to make a tight turn on a small surface and is indicative of the versatility that they possess below ground when hunting.

Ferrets have a good sense of balance and use the tensile grip of their feet with non-retractile claws when climbing.

feet should be bathed in warm water, thoroughly dried and then sprinkled with antiseptic powder. When working your ferret in muddy conditions remember to wash and dry the paws caked in mud as a preventative measure.

Injuries

The most common injury that I have encountered amongst my army of ferrets is that caused to the back by the fall of an over-ambitious and reckless climber. My ferrets love to ascend a variety of objects and show little regard for their own safety once they have set their mind on reaching a certain precipice and sometimes the inevitable happens as they over-stretch themselves and lose their grip. Nowadays this is not a problem because I have made sure there is a soft landing site near every high object, but in my early days of ferret-keeping I saw injury after injury because I was unaware of how readily they will climb and had actually read in a book that they hated to do so.

You only need to look at the animal to realize that the back is the weak link in an otherwise formidable physique and yet it is anatomically perfect for their function as burrow-hunting animals. It is a particularly long vertebral column with little protection and a fall from a minimal height onto a hard surface can cause

irreparable damage as in the case of a polecat jill of mine who had to be put down as a result of her injury. At the least a fall will cause localized bruising and at worst paralysis from damage to the spinal cord.

Following a fall the ferret should be watched carefully to see if it can move and whether that movement is hampered in some form. If the animal can mobilize without too much difficulty and appears more stunned than anything, gently pick it up and massage the affected area to see if it is sensitive to pain. A cold compress can be held against the back to relieve pain if it is present. A ferret which is in obvious distress when moving or trying to move should be taken immediately to the vet who should be required to administer a quick-acting pain-relieving drug to the animal. He will probably want to take an X-ray to determine how serious the injury is and advise you on the best course of action. Any ferret that has suffered a back injury must be supported with both hands when being moved and helped into as comfortable a position as possible. A back injury can take a long time to recover from and the recovery period should not be hurried. A ferret that has suffered a serious back injury will be especially vulnerable to repeat injury in the future and for this reason careful consideration should be given as to

Ferrets seem to be a lot more comfortable when ascending an obstacle and a little hesitant when descending.

whether or not the animal should be retired from rabbiting.

The ferret may incur superficial bite and scratch wounds as a result of mating behaviour, mock battles, during the working of rabbit warrens or when two ferrets that are aggressive towards each other, such as hobs during the breeding season, accidentally meet. Such wounds are easy to spot and are characterized by some localized redness and slight swelling accompanied in some cases with a loss of hair around the wound site. Treatment is relatively simple and can be adequately performed by the ferret keeper. The first task is to assess the severity of the wound and make certain that there are no deep puncture marks present which would require the attention of the vet and probable administration of antibiotics. If there are no puncture marks the cut or scratch should be cleaned regularly with normal saline which is a solution of salt in water and available from the chemist and then covered with a liberal sprinkling of antiseptic wound powder.

Leptospirosis

This condition is more commonly known as Weil's disease and is potentially fatal to man with farmers, sewage workers, fish cutters, vets and hunters being at greatest risk. The disease is usually transmitted via rat's urine or contaminated water. The ferret which has contracted leptospirosis will have a jaundiced or yellow appearance in conjunction with a fever and possible bleeding from the gums. Handle the ferret with caution and either wear disposable gloves or wash your hands thoroughly when touching the animal or litter material. The ferret should be taken immediately to the vet who will be able to treat with antibiotics if the disease has been recognized early enough. If the keeper uses his ferrets for ratting, it is worth his while to consider having his animals vaccinated against leptospirosis.

Mange

Mange is a condition resulting from the presence of external parasites known as *Sarcoptes scabiei*. This nasty microscopic parasite burrows into the outer layer of the skin of the host animal where it lays its eggs. Mange or scab has been known to man as far back as Old Testament times and is mentioned in the book of Leviticus, but it was not until 1619 and the dawn of the microscope that the culprit was actually identified.

Mange first appears on the head and then spreads to the paws and legs as they are used to scratch the head in an effort to relieve the immense irritation that the parasite causes. Within a short space of time the whole body will be infected. Symptoms include loss of hair, redness and thickening of the skin, crust formations, ceaseless scratching and loss of appetite. In its most severe form, mange can cause the death of the host as in the case of foxes which have been known to enter people's houses through cat flaps in their desperate search for warmth.

We first encountered mange some years ago when a Boxer dog bought for my mother lost more than half her coat and was diagnosed by the vet as being a very severe case. He was not very optimistic about the success of treatment, but gave my mother a shampoo and advised her to apply it three to four times a week. Ever one to follow instructions, my mother proceeded to shampoo the dog every day and when the Boxer was taken back to the vet, he was incredulous because the condition was nearly cleared up and he went on to write an article on the treatment of mange based upon my mother's liberal application of the shampoo.

If a ferret contracts mange it should be taken to the vet and treated intensively. When there is substantial hair loss and during the cold weather

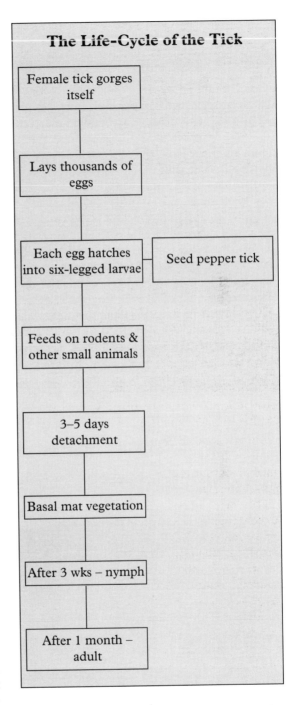

The Life-Cycle of the Tick

Female tick gorges itself

Lays thousands of eggs

Each egg hatches into six-legged larvae

Seed pepper tick

Feeds on rodents & other small animals

3–5 days detachment

Basal mat vegetation

After 3 wks – nymph

After 1 month – adult

the ferret should be placed under a low-intensity broody lamp so as to maintain its body heat. The ferret should be isolated so that the mange does not spread and a high-energy diet offered.

Ticks

The most common parasite with which we have had to deal when rescuing ferrets that have endured a spell of wild living is the tick. When I took home a large polecat hob which had raided a nearby house and slaughtered the guinea pigs, my brother and I counted fourteen ticks that were feeding on the poor creature's blood. They could be seen behind the ears, on the neck, around the tops of the legs and down the back and were at different stages of engorgement.

Of the two families of tick, it is the so-called 'hard' ticks which affect the ferret. They are given this title because they have a hard shield that protects their dorsal region which is why they are difficult to squash between the fingers. These are also ticks that need three hosts. That is they have three active stages in their life cycle and during each of these stages the tick needs to attach itself to a mammal and feed upon its blood. These three stages are larva, nymph and adult with a moulting taking place on the ground between each one. From their position on the ground ticks climb the long blades of grass and await the passage of an animal in anticipation of cementing their mouth parts firmly to its limbs.

Ticks may adversely affect the ferret by caus-ing anaemia, distress or wounds filled with pus and should be dealt with immediately upon discovery. There are two ways to deal with the tick which are either to remove it or apply a substance to the body of the tick, so that it dies and falls off the host animal. To remove the tick the keeper requires a good pair of tweezers and absolute certainty that he can remove the head as well as the body of the tick because a head that is left *in situ* will produce a nasty and unnecessary sore. If the tick is too small to remove or the keeper doubts his ability to extract the head of the tick, vaseline or a neutral gel should be applied to all the visible parts of the tick which will die due to oxygen starvation and give up its hold on the ferret. This is a safe, effective and sure method of dealing with ticks which should be placed in a jar of paraffin as soon as they are removed from or fall off the ferret.

Nursing the Sick Ferret

As I approached the ferret cage that contained my prize polecat hob Romulus, I noticed that he was not anticipating my arrival as usual. In fact he was very lethargic and had to be pulled out of the sleeping box. He was listless and

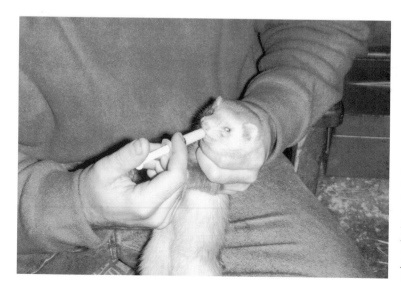

A syringe full of rehydration fluid can be administered slowly to a malnourished ferret. By placing the hand around the neck to hold the ferret, the handler will be able to feel the working swallowing reflex of the animal. If this cannot be felt, all feeding should stop immediately and the vet consulted.

displayed no interest in his food or drink and looked to all intents and purposes as if he would not make it through another night.

This is a description of the classical behaviour of a sick ferret. It will not want to move, but to rest and the first lesson that the keeper should learn is not to disturb the ailing ferret constantly, but to allow it to have plenty of sleep in between interventions. Lack of food is not a major problem and should not be worried about at this stage, but fluid intake is a different matter and is vital. On this particular occasion, Romulus would barely drink even if I offered him his favourite fluid. Consequently, I equipped myself with a syringe and slowly dripped rehydration fluid into his mouth giving him about ten millilitres at one time. This must be done slowly and only when the keeper is sure that the ferret is swallowing normally. A suitable formula for rehydration fluid that will promote recovery can be made from half a teaspoon of salt and one tablespoon of glucose mixed in one pint of tepid water.

A characteristic of sickness in any animal is the inability to continue functioning as normal and the keeper will notice that the sick ferret will not rise to use its familiar litter corner. Therefore the nest often becomes soiled and must be cleaned regularly as well as the ferret itself if need be. Extra bedding material or a broody lamp should be utilized to help maintain an even temperature for the ferret.

Nursing the ferret is fundamentally concerned with doing everything possible to relieve the suffering of a sick and distressed animal. Some actions are obvious and others ordered by the vet, some are to do with simply keeping the ferret clean and warm while others may include administering prescribed antibiotics by sub-cutaneous injections. I have always endeavoured to do the best for my ferrets irrespective of what malady may strike them and by nursing them in the manner described above have seen some quite rapid recoveries.

The Role of the Vet

Ferret keepers are not renowned for taking their animals to the vet and are quite proficient at do-it-yourself remedies that have in the past and continue nowadays to work wonders. However, vets do have specialized knowledge and an array of drugs at their disposal to deal with infection and pain, and the skill of an experienced ferret-keeper lies in knowing when he does need the help of the vet.

The most common reason for my ferrets going to the vet's is for convenience surgery, namely the castration of entire hobs. The vet also has a role as diagnostician and can help to confirm the keeper's suspicions about his ferrets and initiate a plan of effective treatment. The saddest reason for consulting the vet is when an animal has reached the height of its suffering and must be put down to relieve it of its struggle. The ferret like every other animal has the right to have its life ended in a quick and non-traumatic fashion and drugs are the best way to achieve this.

When taking a ferret to the vet the keeper should go equipped with a full history of his animal and what particular changes he has noticed in it that are causing him concern. The more information that is given, the easier the task of the vet becomes.

5 BREEDING THE FERRET

Reasons for Breeding

It may be helpful to start this section by stating that making money is not a good incentive for breeding ferrets for the following reasons. The average price of a ferret is around £5, markedly less than the cost of feeding kits, not to mention the investment of time that should be spent handling and socializing them. Secondly, due to the size of large litters, it is difficult to find a suitable home for every kit and the breeder will often end up with the responsibility of caring for the animals into early adulthood and even beyond. It is impossible to predict how many kits a litter will contain. There are always a large number of ferrets available following the commencement of the breeding season, many of which have been bred by keepers who have built a reputation for providing annual youngsters to those who want them. Thirdly, a lot of avid ferreters breed their own animals in a quest to replicate certain characteristics and continue a specific strain.

Neither is it essential to breed ferrets in order to maintain the health of the jill. The supposition that an unmated jill will not survive the breeding season is a hypothesis that has been continuously disproved by keepers who possess elderly jills that have never been mated. The seasonal changes in appearance, loss of weight and thinning of the coat that are seen in the jill are mistakenly thought of as a loss of condition when in actuality they are the animal's natural hormonal responses. Furthermore, these changes and apparent loss of condition must take place in order for the animal to become pregnant. The act of mating does not stop these occurrences, but merely lessens their duration. An unmated jill will survive quite happily if conscientious management is provided and it is certainly no more difficult to pull it through the breeding season than it is to care for the post-natal jill and her newborn. I have never had a mortality amongst my unmated jills that could be attributed to them not being bred from, but if you are in doubt and have ferrets from which you have no intention of breeding, then it is certainly worth considering the convenient surgical procedure of spaying which will prevent any change in condition that the breeding season usually occasions.

The primary reason for breeding is to increase one's current number of ferrets so that there are young workers ready to replace those close to retirement. Other breeders are concerned with the continuation of a certain line of working ferrets or attempting to produce a specific characteristic in the progeny. There is also the option of introducing new blood from a borrowed or recently acquired hob in the hope of improving stock or creating an ever better strain. The breeding of ferrets will complete the keeper's education of his charges and give him experience of all aspects of managing the creatures from an early age. There is a great deal of pleasure to be derived from breeding one's own animals and using a working ferret which is the product of one's own breeding programme.

Who and When?

If a keeper after careful thought decides that breeding is the best option for him, he must

When choosing a ferret to breed from, the keeper should ensure that the animal is free from obvious defects and possesses a pleasant and amiable disposition.

review his current stock and select suitable candidates for breeding. The candidates selected will depend upon the system of breeding chosen which can be either mating like to like, inbreeding, line-breeding or mating unlikes. Whichever system is used, the same basic criteria are applicable as a guideline for choosing the individual ferrets to be bred from. Each animal should be in the best possible condition and free from obvious disabilities and maladies. They should each possess excellent characters and have proved themselves reliable in the field of work. Parents should be chosen with a view to complementing each other, improving each other's weak points and strengthening and fixing good points. If a particular characteristic such as coat colour or physique is desired this should be borne in mind when choosing the hob and jill for breeding.

As the daylight hours get longer and the weather becomes warmer the keeper will notice changes in the physical appearance and behaviour of his animals that signal the beginning of the breeding season, usually in about March or April. The reproductive organ of the jill and testicles of the hob increase dramatically in size and become overtly obvious. Behaviourally, the hobs will be preoccupied to the point of obsession with mating and will become aggressive in their overtures to other entire hobs to such an extent that they must be housed and exercised separately. However, in my experience hobs living with castrated males or hobbles as they are known may live peaceably together throughout the summer. The jills are frantically restless, running up and down endlessly and are apt to become a bit intolerant of handling and may display some aggressive behaviour. Jills that are usually housed together sometimes fall out with one another during the breeding season and although not doing any real harm to one another are best kept apart.

I like to breed from animals that have a previous knowledge of one another and have lived together throughout the winter. I will leave the animals together until the jill shows the characteristic signs that a successful mating has taken place – these include a reduction in the size of the vulva, appearance of weight gain and nest building activities. Once these signs are apparent, the hob is whisked off to a new home while the jill remains in her familiar environment so that she may concentrate on making a nest in which to have the litter.

The mating ritual is rough, unromantic, noisy and prolonged. The hob will seize the jill by the scruff of the neck and drag her ruthlessly about inducing ovulation before mounting. Most people leave the hob and jill together for a minimum of a couple of days to increase the probability of successful mating. Ferrets are polygamous and fervent in their endeavours to breed and for this reason entire hobs and unmated jills must be kept separate unless kits are required. Ferrets reach sexual maturity during their first season, but I prefer to breed from an animal that is at least two years of age because I will already have seen her through one breeding season and so can more accurately predict her behaviour, which will aid handling following the birth. I also believe that it takes a reasonable amount of time to get to know a ferret's character and capabilities in depth and feel that an animal can be better assessed with regard to breeding purposes when you have observed it through the four seasons of one year.

The Pregnant Jill

Following a successful mating, the jill's swelling will drastically reduce and she will display a shape and weight gain that further confirms her condition of being with kit. A period of approximately forty days will elapse before the kits are delivered during which time the breeder must show informed care for his animal which will contribute to the well-being of the mother-to-be and normal development of the kits *in utero*. Some years ago, when I first embarked on breeding my own ferrets, I was delighted with the mating of two favoured polecats and anxious to do all in my power to secure a happy end to this beginning. I had heard worrying tales of kits aborted by over-protective jills who resented the constant disturbance of prying eyes, not to mention unexplained post-natal deaths and resolved to do little other than make minor alterations to the normal routine of the jill and watch with hope as nature took its course.

The in-young jill needs a safe environment, adequate diet and access to exercise which is the responsibility of the keeper to provide and in return for which he should receive a healthy litter of kits. I am a great believer in creating as little change as possible to the life and environment to which the jill is accustomed and for this reason will decide a season in advance which animal I intend to breed from and consequently house her in a cage suitable for giving birth and rearing kits in. The main feature that I will look for in a breeding cage is a sleeping box that is well separated from the rest of the cage and will support the nest that is built within it. The sleeping box must offer the jill privacy and provide her with the assurance that it is safe. The breeding cage should be placed in a peaceful position where there will be the minimum of noise and disturbance. If the keeper is of a nature that cannot resist the temptation to spy upon a mother with her newborn, it is worth his while building features into the cage that enable him to observe them without disrupting them. There is the option of making a concealed pop hole or replacing the roof of the nesting box

Steps to Successful Breeding.

Breed from good stock only

|

Separate the hob from the
jill following mating

|

Feed the jill well during gestation and
increase her diet/fluid intake as necessary

|

Exercise the jill daily in a safe environment

|

Provide sufficient bedding material for
the jill to make a nest

|

Keep other ferrets and animals away from
the jill's cage

|

Interfere with the jill as little as possible
during the birth and for the first 3–4 weeks
post-natally

nant jill to be housed with other females of the species and these can remain together until the fifth week of pregnancy when they should be removed. However, I prefer to accommodate the jill separately following the removal of the hob because she will have fewer changes to adjust to and will not have to compete for food.

Every effort should be made to maintain as normal a life as possible for the mother-to-be. Her usual routine should be continued and access to exercise made readily available. For the pregnant rabbiting ferret the question of whether or not to work does not arise because the traditional rabbiting season will have already drawn to a close. However, if the keeper decides to ferret out of season he would be well advised to refrain from working a pregnant jill because of the increase in temperature and discomfort experienced by the animal in the warm weather. I have considered it wise practice to supervise closely the exercise of pregnant jills in order to arrest their reckless attempts at jumping and climbing which place the developing kits in jeopardy.

An appetizing and well-balanced diet is required by the jill during the gestation period that will enable her to supply from her own bloodstream the constituents necessary for the formation and growth of the bones, muscles and entire bodies of the kits which can number as few as two to as many as fourteen. During the past I have given my pregnant jills their normal diet of day-olds and replacement milk which has kept them in first class condition throughout the gestation period, but be prepared to offer larger portions as the pregnancy progresses. The diet of choice must contain copious amounts of bone and body-building foods together with vitamins necessary for health and essential minerals. The diet will provide the animal with regular bowel function and those foods should be avoided that have a tendency to cause constipation. Regular elimination is vital in order to deal with the waste products of both the mother and her litter.

As the pregnancy nears its completion, the jill

with one that is made of perspex, however, if these alterations were used, the cages would have to be placed within another structure for protection.

The amorous hob should be removed from the jill once the keeper is satisfied that the hob has accomplished his task and thereafter all hobs should be prevented from having access to the pregnant jill. It is not unusual for a preg-

will show less interest in performing her daily routine, less desire to be handled and more diligence towards nest-building and resting. Do not be surprised if she displays a thinning of the coat because it is quite common for her to use some of her own hair to line the nest. After a minimum of thirty-eight days from the time of conception, the jill will enter the nest and give birth to the kits which she has been carrying. She will deliver them quite naturally without request or requirement for help and any good-natured interference at this stage will be resented by the ferret and may abort an otherwise successful birth. The keeper should wait for the obvious signs of a birth having taken place – for example, the mother will show a loss of weight and shape around the abdomen, together with faster and more excitable movement. Also, by listening carefully, one should be able to discern the bleating of newborn kits, especially when the jill is feeding or exercising outside the nest. Consequently, there is no need to intrude into the nest which can only cause distress to the protective jill.

Like weasels, stoats and polecats, the ferret makes an attentive and fiercely protective parent and should be treated with understanding and respect. The nursing mother will be preoccupied with attending to her offspring and will only emerge from the nest to feed, drink and use her toilet area. When she does come out of the nest the keeper has the opportunity to gently pick her up and examine her condition quickly. One should check that the teats of the animal are functional and being used, that she is of reasonable weight and there is no sign of copious discharge from the reproductive organ. This must only take a couple of minutes and then the jill should be allowed to return to her nest. Any longer and she will begin to show signs of distress at being away from her brood and cannot be blamed for becoming aggressive to the hand that restrains her.

As with the rest of the pregnancy the role of the keeper is to observe his animals and continue to look after their fundamental biological needs. If all appears well, leave well alone, but if the jill shows signs of fading or the bleating of the kits can no longer be heard after careful and regular listening, further investigation must be carried out.

A New Mouth to Feed

Having observed and cared for a pregnant jill for a period of six weeks, the keeper breathes a sigh of relief when the sound of squeaking kits can be heard indicating that a successful and uncomplicated birth has taken place. However, it is not time for him to relax his concentrated regime of care because he must continue to care for a jill who has undergone considerable physical and hormonal changes and upon whose body is placed the additional burden of providing milk and security for the post-natal kits. Perinatally there is little for the keeper to

A four-week-old kit held by the scruff of the neck in the same way as the parent carries it.

At one week old, kits' eyes and ears are sealed, but they have grown a thin white coat since the naked state of their birth.

do but ensure that the environment – that is the birthing cage which should have been placed in position and housed the jill from at least her conception onwards – remains quiet and free from unusual potentially stressful stimuli and a wide variation in temperature. Although it may sound somewhat contradictory, the best that the keeper can do for the jill perinatally is to leave well alone and allow the animal's natural process of birth and the early development of the kits to take place uninterrupted. Too many cases have been recounted in which kit death has been attributed to the owner's inability to resist visual and tactile checking of the jill when her instincts crave the privacy from which she derives her feelings of security.

Post-natally, the jill should be checked daily to ensure that she is maintaining weight, producing milk and is alert and contented.

Appetite should be observed and any alterations in dietary intake made. She will continue to require feeding twice a day and I continue to offer my ferrets calcium and vitamin-rich ewe's replacement milk.

When my first litter was born I used to routinely stand by the cage and listen for signs of kit life four times a day and sometimes more and would suggest checking at least three times a day – for example, in the morning, at midday and during the evening. This will assure the keeper that all is well and does not take up much time at all. The keeper must remember that the mustelid kit is born naked and with eyes and ears tightly sealed and therefore will be totally dependent upon the mother for the warmth, food and protection that is imperative for the continuance of its life. The keeper can help to achieve this by having given forethought to the

A one-week-old kit in the hand, displaying its small size and defenceless state. Not surprisingly the jill will be very protective.

siting of the breeding cage, to providing sufficient nest material and supplying the diet and fluids that a new mother will need in order to be able to produce the milk craved by the kits.

Daily I would go through the motions of stopping by the cage, listening for signs of life, checking the health of the jill and placing food and fluids in the cage for her satisfaction. As I did so, the squeaking of the kits became louder and louder as they increased their movement within the nest until one day towards the end of the second week a small lightly furred head appeared that was hastily retrieved with great alacrity as the mother secured hold of her offspring by the nape of its neck. This is an encouraging sign because it displays the development of maternal instincts which means that the kits will be retrieved to the warmth of

the nest despite their crawling. Once the kits begin to appear with some regularity, the keeper can consider putting some food in for them which will start to wean them off the mother's milk. The food should be soft in order to be digested and I provided my kits with day-olds that I had minced immediately prior to giving. As they still have their eyes sealed they may need pointing in the right direction for their food and they will often clamber into the midst of the bowl full of food and have bloodstained fur by the time they have finished eating, but the mother will clean them up admirably once they have returned to the nest. I also offered them ewe's replacement milk in an effort to reduce the strain on the mother. I fed my kits two to three times a day and was able to monitor their appetite and weight. The jill was also happy for

During the third week the kit's eyes are still sealed and the movement uncoordinated.

A hand-operated mincer is used to soften and mash up large portions of food so that they are suitable for consumption by kits. This introduces them to the food that is to be their staple diet, thus eliminating the need to buy special provisions.

A five-week-old kit exploring its surroundings.

This five-week-old kit is much more certain in its movements and already has the familiar shape of the adult ferret.

Three lively seven-week-old albino kits of a total litter of six enjoy exercise in a run during the summer weather.

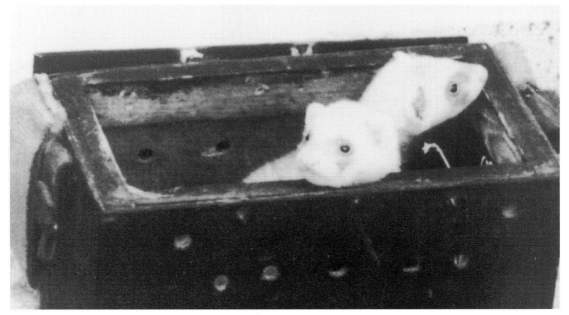

I like to get my kits used to the carrying box from an early age.

me at this time to begin gently handling her offspring and familiarizing them with the hand of their keeper.

As the teeth developed and the chewing action became more proficient I gave the kits meat which was less finely minced than their previous feeds and progressively provided them with more substance to chew on until they could reasonably cope with an entire day-old. By this time – approximately the fourth week, the eyes and ears begin to open and the opening of the eyes at slightly different times provides the kit with a comical appearance.

By the fifth week the kits will have become increasingly active and the mother will have difficulty in keeping them within the nest. Once they have reached this stage they are ready to start exercising in different and more interesting environments than the cage. I usually exercise young kits on my ferret-shed floor or if the weather is agreeable place them in an outside run with some pipes and other objects to play with. It is my practice to oversee their exercise and combine it with handling and familiarization.

The taming and handling of kits should be confident and gentle and some nipping is to be expected as they learn about the world with their teeth. They will soon realize what they should and should not bite. The successful breeding of my own ferrets and watching the kits mature into adulthood and develop into capable workers has been one of the most rewarding aspects that I have experienced as a keeper.

6 THE RESCUED FERRET

The question the reader is most likely to ask himself is 'Why do ferrets need rescuing?' In common with cats and dogs, ferrets may be lost, ill-treated or unwanted due to a change of mind or unforeseen alteration in circumstances. Unfortunately, the erroneous presumption that a ferret is capable of establishing itself in the wild is still maintained by those who look for an easy option out of their duty of care for the creature and rescuers commonly encounter ferrets which have simply been turned loose to fend for themselves. Over the previous ten years my family and I have been actively involved in the rescue and rehoming of needy ferrets, but we are by no means the first or the only group of people to be concerned at the plight of the ferret.

With the demise of the rabbit industry and the introduction of myxomatosis, the role of the ferret became largely ambiguous and mass numbers were released by owners who could visualize no remaining purpose for what they considered singularly as a working animal. Some of these ferrets did become feral, while others either starved to death or fell prey to other animals. Conscientious keepers became all too aware of this situation and began to take in and rehabilitate those loose and dejected ferrets that appeared in their locality. Consequently, the need to rescue ferrets is by no means a contemporary phenomenon and cannot be levelled at any group other than that band of irresponsible characters who have no real concern for the welfare of the animals that have passed through their hands.

Certain misconceptions have not helped the situation either in the past or at present. These are namely that jills must be bred annually or else they will die and that ferrets are not valuable enough to merit having money spent on them. In addition there is the widespread myth that ferrets are by nature recalcitrant and untrustworthy. None of these suppositions are true and are a poor excuse for breeding unwanted animals or withholding beneficial treatment.

Due to the poor rabbiting following the widespread introduction of myxomatosis the ferret began to take on the role of a pet in the backyard of many former workers and the number of purely pet ferrets has steadily increased as more and more people realized the wealth of character that these little animals have. As with most popular animals increased demand has resulted in the proliferation of breeders, some of whom are interested in the accumulation of money rather than producing healthy well-bred ferrets. On one occasion I met a breeder who informed me that he only had sixty kits left at the end of the season and these were kept in such large numbers that they had to be fiercely competitive for food and were inadequately handled and ironically therefore wholly unsuitable as either pet or working ferrets. Another breeder of whom I became aware was breeding ferrets on the balcony of a high-rise flat in the centre of a major city where they were denied an environment in which they could prosper and exercise properly. Many of these surplus animals have found their way typically to animal shelters.

Most cases of cruelty are based upon blatant ignorance of how to work and care for a ferret. In times past a merciless owner would file the teeth or sew together the jaws of his animal in order to prevent it killing a rabbit in the warren when hunting and such activities, though very rare, are still reported today. It is much more common to find a ferret that is housed in unsuitable accommodation that is of such alarmingly small dimensions that it is considered injurious to health. More often than not this is combined with no handling of the animal or cleaning of the cage and infrequent feeding.

If you go to any of the well-known animal welfare shelters you will quite likely come across at least a handful of ferrets who have been badly mistreated along the lines just mentioned here. There are happily countless regional ferret welfare groups whose members offer a service of care for lost, injured or poorly treated ferrets. Finally, there are the lone rangers who are known to the local community for their eccentric fascination with ferrets and willingness to help any such animal in need.

Our own small ferret rescue happened more by accident than design and was linked to the acquisition of my mongrel bitch combined with regular visits to the nationally known and local animal shelter. My dog, Sally, was a rescue case as a puppy and enabled us to establish links with people who were delighted with our offer to deal with any mustelids that they might come across and we were honestly quite surprised at the number of calls that we received. Another way in which we endeavoured to help the ferret was by providing permanent homes for the animals that had been handed in by one means or another to the animal sanctuary. Whilst I do not have access to statistics regarding the increase or decrease of incidences of the rescue or rehoming of ferrets, I can state from my own observation within the locality in which I used to live, that there was a steady increase in the occurrence of ferrets at the animal shelter.

There is without doubt a need for people who know about and understand the ferret to use their experience and become involved in helping ferrets which may have been lost, are malnourished, afraid and suspicious of humans. To witness the recovery and taming of a sickly ferret is one of the most rewarding experiences I have encountered during my years as an ardent ferret-keeper.

Lost, but not Found

Due to the nature of the traditional fieldsport of ferreting, now and again, a conscientious keeper who thinks the world of his ferrets may encounter a warren which refuses to give back his prized animal and, despite his arduous and tiring efforts, he is forced by the hours of the day to put his trust in a trap and leave the site without his ferret.

As I was out and about ferreting with my brother by a narrow stream we hoped to add to the half dozen rabbits already bagged by working a small well-used warren. As we netted up, the heavens opened and unleashed a downpour of huge rain drops that hurtled with relentless force upon us. We were unperturbed and stiffened our resolve to endure the wet weather for a few minutes more while Ginger, a capable little jill, worked the system following which we would be able to sprint back to the car. Our confidence could not have been more ill judged as Ginger encountered an obdurate rabbit that was not going to bolt come hell or high water. Consequently, Ginger lay up behind the rabbit trying to kill it; however, the tunnel was too narrow to allow the ferret to reach the neck of the rabbit and inflict the mortal wound. Ginger probably received a few powerful blows to the head from the dangerous and powerful hind legs of her quarry.

As time ticked hopelessly by it became obvious to my brother and I that the only option remaining was to commence digging. The incessant monsoon had converted the *terra firma* beneath our feet into a sea of mud and our wellie-shod feet slid painfully in opposite directions as we fought to penetrate the earth with spades which became increasingly harder to grip. After a period of fifteen minutes which seemed like fifteen hours, my brother, who looked like a mud wrestler, had managed to open up the warren revealing its intricate system of tunnels. As we were contemplating which one to follow, we noticed that the little stream had been replaced by a veritable river that was inching its way closer and closer towards us. We were surveying it with disbelief when there was a tumultuous landslide caused by the destabilized warren caving in upon itself and to our dismay Ginger had, so we thought, been irretrievably buried without trace beneath an immense mound of sticky clay soil. This was a rather dramatic and heartbreaking way to lose a ferret, but it plainly shows that most losses whilst out hunting are due to events beyond the ferreter's control. To our relief we were able to retrieve quite miraculously a muddy and bedraggled Ginger on our return visit to the site the following morning, but not everyone is blessed with such good fortune. The lesson clearly is to do all that is within your power on the day of the loss and then return to the site as often as possible for as many as several weeks following the loss of a ferret. On another occasion we had to abandon a ferret due to failing light and did not see hide or hair of the animal for an entire week until a friendly farm worker informed us of a sighting which led to a hasty retrieval of a hungry ferret.

The other major cause of losing ferrets derives from an inaccurate assessment of the creature's ability to perform the role of escapologist. Ferrets can tear apart chicken wire with little effort, they can climb and squeeze their bodies through minute spaces and once they have made up their mind to follow a certain path they remain totally concentrated on the task in hand. They are more likely to attempt escapes during the breeding season for obvious reasons. Due to the fact that I have always and continue to exercise my animals unrestrained in open spaces I have experienced, when my back is momentarily turned, some heart-stopping episodes during which a ferret's wanderings have taken it completely out of sight. On such occasions the family is quickly summoned to initiate a search, and we have had a few eventful ones where ferrets have been retrieved from a path by a main road or have routed around the farm by themselves for up to half an hour. I have a hob called Thunder for reasons best kept to myself who wanders endlessly by himself without getting lost and appears to have the instincts of a homing pigeon for returning to the ferret shed. The jills are a lot more reckless and must be watched like a hawk.

The final reason for the loss of ferrets results from the owner's decision that he no longer wants the creature and might just as well let it go as trouble himself with finding it a new home. We have had numerous calls to rescue ferrets that have simply been deserted for no other reason than that they have fallen out of favour with their previous owners.

The Capture of a Ferret

The capture of a ferret may either be by one's own physical action in terms of actually securing a grip on the lost animal or it may involve setting a live trap. We have been called out many times to rescue ferrets from people's wood sheds, coal bunkers, backyards and gardens. On some occasions capturing the ferret is a simple matter of walking over and picking the animal up, but sometimes when the ferret is injured, angry or frightened a good deal of caution must be displayed in order to prevent either injury to the rescuer or the ferret taking flight. The first priority of the rescuer is to assess the environment in which the rescue is to take place and the condition of the ferret. Take the time to block potential escape routes and observe the animal closely so that you know what you are dealing with because you may find that what is supposed to be a ferret is in fact a stoat or weasel. Prepare the carrying box in which you intend to place the ferret and put on a sturdy gauntlet.

Approach the ferret carefully talking to it gently as you get closer. If it remains relatively still, squat down and make an inviting noise for it at the same time as offering the hand with the gauntlet on. If the animal has been previously well handled it will allow you to secure a hold

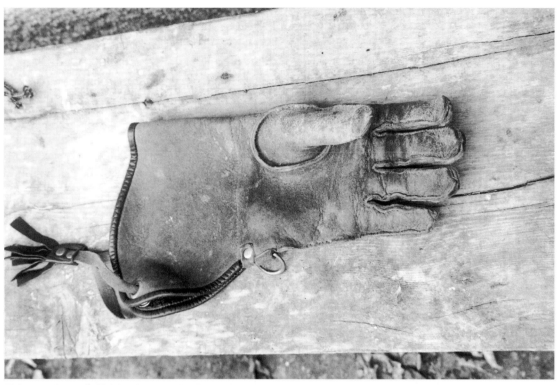

Falconry glove. A thick leather gauntlet designed to protect the hand from the powerful talons of raptors is ideal for securing hold of an aggressive or nervous ferret and is an invaluable part of the rescuer's equipment.

on it and go calmly into the carrying box. However, the ferret may not have been well handled, but could have been wild for a considerable time, close to starving or in pain. If as you move towards the ferret it hisses, fans out its tail or begins to run you will have a more difficult job on your hands as such an animal is much more likely to bite and evade your attempts at capture. In such cases use appetizing food or a bowl of milk to entice the animal into the open where a decisive movement with the arm will grab hold of the ferret. Alternatively, you may use a sturdy net on a long pole or if all else fails bait a live trap and beat a retreat until the ferret is caught. A rescuer must be decisive in choosing the best option for capture and reinforce his plan with positive movements.

I always take a gauntlet with me to recover a lost and strange ferret because it may be hell bent on biting me and the last thing that I want to do is draw back my hand and be hesitant. My first pair of gauntlets were purchased at the local ironmongers for approximately £11 and had a sufficient thickness of leather covering the palms and fingers to prevent the teeth of a ferret penetrating the skin. The gauntlets must be thick enough to stop the teeth going through, but supple enough to allow the ferret to be felt through them and heavy-duty garden or welder's gloves will do the job admirably. A more expensive, but probably the best option is to buy a single-thickness falconry glove which should cost in the region of £30 and if well looked after will outlast those already mentioned. These gloves are designed to protect the hand from the awesome and powerful talons of raptors and are more than a match for an aggressive ferret. I am aware that books advise keepers not to handle ferrets with gloves on, but they are not referring to rescue situations and it is far more prudent to be safe than sorry. Once the ferret is successfully caught place it in a secure carrying box in which it can be transported to a safe environment for a thorough check over.

Not so Splendid Isolation

Unless the rescued ferret is in need of immediate veterinary attention, such as when shot or wounded in some manner, it should be taken to a holding cage located well away from the rescuer's own ferrets. This is principally to isolate the animal and prevent the risk of spreading the parasites that are likely to be resident on its body as well as provide a quiet environment from which the ferret can derive a sense of security. Isolation is also a precaution against the spread of other more serious problems such as distemper or mange, but it is only beneficial if you remember to wash your hands carefully after each handling, wear a carpenter's apron whilst cleaning the cage and keep any bowls or utensils separate. I must stress that none of the many ferrets that I have rescued were suffering from viral or ectoparasitic infections and were segregated in order to deal with common fleas and ticks. Should you suspect a serious infection collaborate with your vet who will advise you on infection control measures such as wearing disposable gloves and how to safely destroy litter.

From the ferret's point of view, being caged separately means that it will not have to compete for any of its fundamental needs, primarily food, and will have the opportunity to recover full health and vigour before having to integrate and make friends with other ferrets. If the animal is undergoing any veterinary treatment, this should be completed prior to caging it with other ferrets. It is also beneficial for the new owner to have the ferret used to being handled and understand its general character

before ending the isolation period. Ideally, at the completion of the isolation the ferret keeper should be able to introduce a healthy, tame and adjusted animal to his existing stock.

Health Check Assessment for the Rescued Ferret

Upon initially taking a rescued ferret to an isolation cage it is vital that a simple, but thorough assessment of the creature's health be undertaken in order to highlight any needs it may have and initiate an appropriate plan of care. The assessment chart gives an idea of what to look for and what action to take when examining the ferret from head to tail. It is helpful to have somebody hold the animal while you closely scrutinize it and remember to wear your gauntlets as a precaution because you will still be quite a stranger to the bewildered animal. You should basically be looking to see if the rescued ferret can move, breathe, eat, hear, see and defecate in a normal manner.

Care of the Malnourished Ferret

With the exception of the treatment of the loathsome fleas and ticks already mentioned the most common problem that I have encountered amongst rescued ferrets is malnutrition accompanied by a reduction in the mean body mass. I have seen ferrets that have been literally all skin and bone and have myself come up with a diet for weight gain based upon that given to a ferret of my own breeding, aptly called Mouse, who seemed incapable of maintaining a healthy minimum weight. Even a visit to the vet and an injection could not encourage the little character to bulk out, but the vet agreed that the basic diet of day-old chicks, fresh water and replacement milk should prove adequate. Fed up with looking at and feeling his thin physique, I went off to the local supermarket and returned home armed with tins of evaporated milk and rice pudding. I mixed two measures of

Assessment Chart

Anatomical Feature	Assessment	Action
Mouth	Check for a normal pink colour and healthy teeth	If the mouth is pale treat for shock (vet)
Nose	Observe discharge	Clean with tepid water Refer to vet if it does not clear within 48 hrs
Eyes	Should be bright and alert	Remove any foreign bodies Refer to vet
Ears	Note blockages or bleeding	Refer to vet Administer ear drops
Coat	Check matting for parasites and mange	Refer to Ch. 4 Comb and shampoo
Feet	Look for foot rot	Refer to Ch. 4
Skin	Observe for wounds Test for dehydration	Clean and cover with powder or honey Give rehydration fluid
Limbs	Test for function Obvious breaks	If there is pain, apply cold compress Refer to vet
Claws	Curling over	Clip carefully

evaporated milk to every one measure of rice pudding and presented Mouse with a small bowlful every day which he lapped up with absolute delight. To see Mouse today, you would not believe he is the same ferret as that pitiful figure who never gained weight and it has been suggested, albeit rather tongue in cheek, that two hands are now required to lift him. Combined with a meat feed, the provision of evaporated milk and rice pudding is terrific for producing substantial and healthy weight gain and the frequency and size of portions can be varied to suit the ferret's particular needs.

If a ferret has difficulty with solids, the meat can be minced or the animal can start off on some beef tea that was, in years gone by, used in sick-room cookery for human patients and considered to have all the qualities of a reparative and nourishing food, easily absorbable by delicate stomachs. I have a recipe from 1898 which uses a quarter of a pound of lean juicy beef, a quarter of a pint of cold water and a pinch of salt. The beef should be shredded finely and put into a basin with the cold water and salt. Stir it well, cover and let stand for thirty minutes to an hour, stirring it occasionally. When the fluid is bright red it should be put through a fine strainer and the residue placed in a piece of muslin which is twisted to express as much juice as possible. This would last the ferret a good few days and it may be worth using a fraction of the ingredients so that a small quantity is made more often and given while it is fresher.

Tales of Rescue

Guinea Pig for Breakfast

One Saturday morning as I was readying myself to attend to my ferrets a man and his boy who were unknown to me came down the drive looking a little unsure of themselves.

'Are you the man who keeps ferrets?' asked the gentleman.

I nodded, not wishing too give away to much information until I knew more about the reason behind his inquiry. He could after all be a poultry keeper who had lost half his stock and was looking for someone to blame.

'There is a ferret, well we think it is a ferret, in our guinea pig cage and the ironmonger said you might be able to help,' he continued.

I assured him that none of my ferrets were missing and my offer to go and have a look at the animal for him was quickly accepted.

In this gentleman's large garage there was what can only be described as a rickety structure that bore a very slight resemblance to a cage. Curled up inside the cage looking as content as can be was a short, stocky, sable ferret with the last remains of a guinea pig lying beside it. 'Is it a ferret?' asked the boy who was more interested in the unknown killer than his poor departed guinea pig, that would have stood no chance against a hungry ferret.

'Yes,' I replied in my usual descriptive manner.

Both father and son jumped back when I opened the cage door as if I were releasing a man-eating lion and not some over-full ferret that had eaten far too much to put up any sort of fight or flight.

'Would you like to stroke him?' I inquired, holding out the indolent ferret towards the boy who looked at it with wide-eyed excitement. One quick touch with his finger-tips was all he dared venture.

I took the ferret home where my brother and I gave it a good look over and found fourteen large ticks fixed to its body. It was a very gentle and tolerant hob which indicates that somebody had taken the trouble to handle him regularly and kindly and had obviously lost him in unfortunate circumstances. Having roamed free in the wild for some time the ferret seemed unable to provide for himself and therefore launched an assault on domestic stock in an effort to satisfy his hunger. He was soon deloused and settled happily into his new cage. I gave him the name Rikki-tikki-tavi after the mongoose in Rudyard Kipling's *Jungle Book* and he was such a delight to own that even my mother used to handle him regularly and would go and speak to him every morning.

Hungry and Tired

The telephone rang and was answered by my mother who recognized the voice of the farm worker at the other end. He wanted our advice about a ferret that was wandering free around his smallholding eating anything that looked edible. My brother advised him to offer the ferret some food and then place it in a box while its attention was distracted and bring it to us. Several hours elapsed before the farm worker turned up empty handed. He had chased the ferret round and round with a fishing net on a long pole until he eventually caught the emaciated creature and put it in a cardboard box where it was left to its own devices while he carried on with some work. Not surprisingly there was a hole in the cardboard through which the ferret had escaped by the time he returned and so my brother gave him a carrying box that a mink could not escape from and wished him luck.

Evening came and he was back again, but this

time with a tick-infested and cowering albino jill that anticipated being hit every time a hand went towards her. The farm worker was assured that the ticks and weight loss were not a problem that a week's good care would not resolve, but that the animal's fear and lack of trust might take a considerably larger time to overcome. We named the jill Scully because she skulked back to the corner of the cage every time we tried to get hold of her. We soon discovered that if we offered Scully a small bowl of evaporated milk she would rush from her nest box as her belly overcame her fear. Whilst she stood drinking we would stroke her gently so that she might be reassured that we intended her no harm. As soon as the milk was finished she would scuttle back to her nest box until one day Scully decided to remain by the bowl and trust our handling. The farm worker came back to see Scully recently and was delighted to see the healthy, happy and playful ferret that she has become.

From One Rescue to Another

The village in which I used to live was located near a huge animal shelter that provided sanctuary for all manner of animals with great success, but the humble little ferret gave them more trouble than all their dogs put together. My brother was looking around the shelter one day when he noticed that a ferret which had recently been rescued was escaping from its

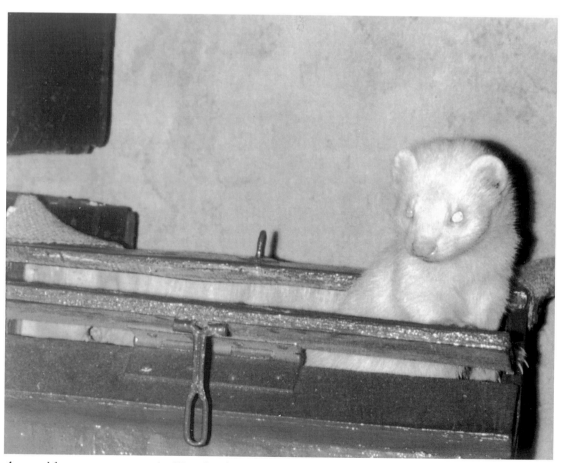

A rescued ferret can recover to enjoy life and make a good working companion.

enclosure and was about to tangle with some cats. Not only did the shelter have problems containing these little beauties, but they also had a horrendous time trying to rehome them and so were very grateful when I offered to take on all the ferrets that they had. One ferret that came from the shelter, previously named Fergus, was without doubt the biggest ferret that I have ever seen and proved to be the typical gentle giant who took everything in his stride.

Becoming Involved in Rescue

Helping to restore the health of a sick animal or the trust of an abused ferret is immensely satisfying and requires little more than incentive, knowledge and time. If a ferret keeper wishes to become involved in rescuing these creatures he can either make himself known to the local animal shelters and rehoming services, contact his nearest ferret welfare club or place a card in the vet's surgery. Being known in the local community and at work also helps and people will bring animals ranging from hedgehogs to rabbits to us for recovery.

Certain preparations should be made before starting to offer your services and these are the provision of adequate cages to put the ferrets in, the acquisition of rescue equipment and a good supply of nourishing food. However, the greatest demand placed upon the rescuer is for his time and he should be absolutely certain that he wants to spend a good deal of his leisure time in the company of ferrets.

7 EQUIPMENT FOR FERRETING

Necessary Items

Ferreting has remained fundamentally unchanged since its earliest days in its practice and effect. The purity of the sport with its accompanying no-nonsense philosophy is one of the features that appealed to my brother and me. However, anybody witnessing many of our ferreting expeditions, once they had stopped reeling with laughter, would have sworn that we had forgotten the past and were attempting to imitate pack horses. Not only have we found such occasions to be tiring and uncomfortable, but totally unnecessary. The increased burdens have intensified the difficulty of negotiating natural and man-made obstacles, sent us sprawling down perilous inclines and hastened a sticky end to our leggings as we attempted to clamber over the dreaded barbed wire in vain. If we have learnt one valuable lesson, it is to take only what equipment is needed for each particular outing. The early ferreters were minimalist in their approach to the sport, taking only purse nets in which to catch the rabbits, net pegs with which to secure the nets and a sack or carrying box in which to transport the ferret. As country partisans they would also have possessed a well and frequently used knife which was treated more like an old friend than an inanimate object and valuable for hocking, gutting and skinning the rabbit.

Purse Nets

The exhilaration and satisfaction experienced when a rabbit is bolted successfully into a preset purse net are familiar to persistent ferreters. Activity below ground is clearly the domain of the reliable working ferret, but the responsibility for capture lies fairly and squarely with the person who has set nets over every exit hole connected to the warren system being worked. The frustration felt when the ferret has worked its little heart out to bolt a rabbit which pushes aside a poorly set net as it explosively leaps into freedom defies verbal expression and is greeted with dumbfounded shoulder shrugging. Consequently, the lesson of taking the required time to set nets precisely is quickly learnt and rather than netting up the holes with a feeling of tedium as if it is only a necessary chore preceding the real undertaking, one is awakened to the realization that the employment of nets in the pursuit of quarry is an art and sometimes a law unto itself. Half the battle of good netsetting is won by the nets themselves which if they are of tiptop construction and design will easily cover exit holes, maintain their position in inclement weather conditions and allow the free movement of the ferret through the mesh spaces.

It is surprising when one realizes the margin of difference that exists between the various rabbit purse nets that are available for purchase depending upon the material from which they are made and the means of production – either by hand or machine. I was awakened to this difference when I attended a local game show many years ago where I encountered an elderly gentleman who had on display an array of hand-made nets strewn over the top of his old Vauxhall. He told my brother and me that they were constructed of marine nylon and that he produced them to generate some extra cash since illness had forced his retirement from

Central to success when ferreting is a supply of purse nets. This picture shows a selection of different length nets suspended from hooks. After each outing in wet weather, nets should be hung so that they can dry without rotting. A thumb stick can be used for support, to investigate holes and to hang nets from when moving short distances.

work. Having spent a considerable amount of our time chatting about the nets and recounting memorable exploits with ferrets, we emptied our pockets of all the money they contained and filled our arms with as many nets as we could buy. Upon returning home we laid our newly acquired nets side by side with the less expensive machine-made ones that my brother had bought previously. They differed in length, weight and shape with the latter being shorter and lighter, which admittedly does not prevent them from being functional in the field, but they will not be so easy to use or last as long as their home-made counterparts.

The two most common materials used in netmaking are hemp and nylon. Hemp is a

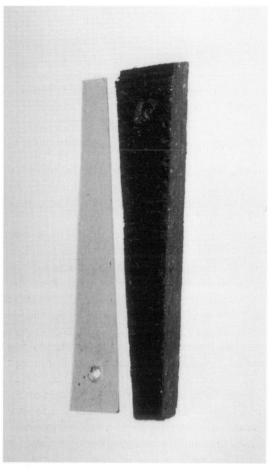

This is a home-made net peg cut from exterior ply and given a good coat of paint for protection. A cardboard template is used so that the pegs are uniform. The drill hole at the top of the peg is for the drawcord and the peg tapers to a narrow point so that it will enter the ground easily.

or load that would have to be placed upon it in order for a break to occur. The great advantage of nylon realized by ferreters is that the material is rot-proof no matter how often it is used in the wettest of conditions and it is also green in colour which eliminates the need to dye nylon nets. I have made nets out of seven-ply polished hemp and 6z spun nylon which have performed equally satisfactorily when used for ferreting. Whether a net is made of hemp or nylon, it is quite common for the drawstring to be made of a braided nylon cord that is fixed to the net peg and usually white in colour. The remaining components of a net are two essential stainless steel rings one inch in internal diameter and to which the net is fixed.

A standard net is of a uniformly straight shape and size which many experienced ferreters believe provides an excess of net at the top and bottom which is not needed to gain a secure purse around a rabbit. Consequently, prudent netmakers started to produce shaped nets which are tapered at the top and bottom, but have a wide mid-section made by adding an extra mesh onto each row until the net centre is reached and then removing them one by one, row after row, until both halves of the net match. The standard net tends to be square when set, while the shaped net is rounded and more akin to the shape of the rabbit holes over which it is set.

The purpose of the nets is to cover every hole leading to and from a rabbit warren and purse around the bolting rabbits. They are vital to the success of any traditional ferreting endeavour and the setting and resetting of nets should be enjoyed by the persistent ferreter. Consequently, one should approach the purchase of purse nets circumspectly and look for features such as the quality of the material and construction that should promote efficacious and enduring use. With this in mind I have compiled a short guide to net buying that can be quickly referred to (*see* opposite).

Net Pegs

In order to work successfully nets must be fixed to a sturdy object which does not move when

natural fibre and is graded according to the number of strands or ply that it contains. As a natural fibre it has been around for a considerable time and has proved to be a great favourite amongst ferreters, both past and present, despite the fact that it will eventually rot unless the nets are treated and hung to dry after they are used in wet conditions. On the other hand, nylon is a man-made material of incredible strength graded according to the breaking strain

A Guide to Buying Nets

Ensure that it is made of either 4–7 ply polished hemp or 4z–6z spun nylon.

The drawcord should be braided nylon and the rings stainless steel.

The net itself should slide freely down the drawcord.

The knots should be secure and pulled tight.

Check the size and number of the mesh spaces. A net should be a minimum of 19 mesh spaces long and 18 mesh spaces wide at the broadest part.

Look for special features such as a shaped net or one that is double stranded.

the force of the rabbit causes the net to purse. A simple and effective way to achieve this is to fix the running cord of the net to a piece of wood which can be driven into the ground. These are known as net pegs and come in a variety of shapes, sizes and materials. The most commonly occurring net peg is made of purchased hardwood, measures between 10–15 cm in length and tapers to a point to make it easier to drive into the ground. However, the oldest type of net peg is made of hazel collected from the woods which after being left to season for at least a year is whittled into shape. The newest net pegs are made of metal or moulded plastic and are manufactured for use by campers, but have also been found to be of some use for securing purse nets.

Each type of net peg has its advantages and disadvantages in varying degree. The hardwood pegs of manufactured wood can be bought ready-made or made by the keeper and are inexpensive whichever option is chosen. They are long-lasting and easy to use presenting a broad

top upon which to apply pressure to drive them into the ground. However, if they are struck with too much force they are liable to break. Natural seasoned hardwood stakes will last for many years if made properly and can withstand the rough treatment that a peg must endure. For these, the ferreter will need access to a supply of natural timber, possess knowledge about which wood to choose and be able to correctly identify the different trees. It will take some time to collect a selection of shanks from which to make the pegs and even longer for them to season so patience and planning must be exercised. The main disadvantage of such pegs is the fact that they cannot be made or used until well seasoned and so are not a good option for the beginner who has just purchased a number of nets and wants to peg them. It is also worth remembering that if your preference is for obtaining pegs in this fashion, you should be continually collecting year after year so that there are always seasoned pegs to replace old or broken ones. Metal or moulded plastic pegs intended for campers are cheap and easy to buy and can be driven into the ground quite easily, but I have found that in icy weather when the ground is extremely hard my ham-fisted approach usually results in a bent or broken peg and therefore I restrict the use of such pegs to soft ground.

Whatever material is selected by the keeper an ideal net peg should be:

1. Easy to drive into the ground in all conditions.
2. Secure once driven into the ground.
3. Able to withstand harsh weather and rough handling.
4. Easy to fix a net to.
5. Lightweight and easy to pack into a game bag.

The usual method for fixing the net to the peg is to drill a hole in the broadest part of the top of the peg through which the braided draw cord can be threaded and then tied into a knot to hold it secure. As has been stated, the net peg is a vital part of the ferreting equipment because it enables the correct and fruitful use of the net and although being plain, simple and cheap thought should be given by the ferreter as to which type of peg will best suit the ground upon which he works.

Carrying Boxes

The ferreter will need to either make or purchase a sturdy wooden box in which the ferret can be transported and contained when moving from one warren to another and laying nets respectively. In the early to mid-twentieth century sacks were in common use for carrying the ferrets to the hunting site. The advantages of these were their light weight, and ready and cheap availability, but they did not offer the animal a secure environment or much protection from the harshness of winter weather. A persistent ferret is also able to chew its way out of a sack and should the keeper inadvertently fall headlong he may well end up with disconsolate animals. Other bags were tried in an effort to overcome these drawbacks, but had little continuous appeal and were replaced by the much more popular and practical wooden carrying boxes.

Without exception, all the ferreters whom I have met use carrying boxes for the transport of their animals. Boxes have become the item of choice because of their strength and ability to withstand the weather. Boxes can be bought from fieldsport suppliers, but in most cases are hand-made according to the keeper's individual design. The box should be made with the aim of satisfying both the ferret that must travel in it and the ferreter who must carry it. The box should be spacious enough for the ferret to move around in and make a nest, be well-ventilated and give protection from the elements. For the carrier, the box must be of light construction and have a comfortable strap making it an easy burden during the trekking that goes hand in hand with a day in the field. Suitable material for a box is exterior ply of a quarter to half an inch in thickness. There is a multitude of designs in which the dimensions

are variable, but the minimum size of a box in which a medium-sized ferret is to be carried is 12in long and 6in in height and width. When purchasing or making a box avoid those which are large and unwieldy and bear in mind that during the course of the day a ferreter may walk a minimum of two miles over awkward terrain.

Knives

I have recollections of my holidays as a youngster when one of the most interesting environments ripe for exploration was my grandfather's workshop in which he had an impressive collection of gardening implements. Included in this were sharpening stones and

A collection of transporters. The traditional wooden carrying box can be home-made, is very strong and most suitable for use when working ferrets during the winter. They should have ventilation holes and can have either a single or split lid. Plastic carriers are suitable for summer transportation and for leaving the ferrets in for longer periods because of the extra space, more light and grid front from which water bottles can be hung.

innumerable pocket knives which had been collected over the years. The main tasks for which he used a knife were to clean his pipe of tobacco, for pruning and for cutting vegetables, but like all countrymen he constantly carried a pocket knife so that it was always ready to hand. A good-quality, well-crafted knife will soon endear itself to the owner and find plenty of uses.

Anyone who is buying a knife for rabbiting must bear in mind what the knife will be used for and in what conditions. The most common use of the ferreter's knife is for hocking rabbits' legs so that they may be carried more easily and for penetrating the abdominal wall so that the rabbit can be paunched. Most rabbiters also use their knives when skinning the carcass. It is worth remembering that ferreting is a winter sport and therefore the equipment of the hunter must be suitable for safe use in both wet and dry weather conditions. Therefore, when purchasing a knife the rabbiter should have in mind safety and look for a handle that can be gripped comfortably when wet or dry and that will prevent the fingers slipping forward onto the blade. The blade should be made of stainless as opposed to carbon steel because it is easier to clean, does not mark and in my experience holds a better edge. The hunter will also benefit from having a blade-locking mechanism incorporated in his knife because it will eradicate completely the possibility of the blade clamping on the fingers.

A small selection of suitable rabbiting knives. On the right is a Victorinox knife which my brother has used daily for the previous ten years. The blades are stainless steel and include a clip point for skinning. The wood saw is particularly useful for clearing small branches out of the way. In the middle is a typical hunting knife made in Japan featuring a lock, stainless steel clip point blade and excellent rubber grip. Some hunters prefer a sheath knife such as the one on the left because you do not have to bother opening the blade. This one has a wooden handle, stainless steel blade and is made in Finland.

It is often said that the only dangerous knife is a blunt one which emphasizes the need to keep the blade sharp. There are many modern devices designed to achieve this, but in my opinion the traditional method of using a quality sharpening stone is best although there is a definite knack to it which can only be acquired by practice. It is imperative that you hold the knife at the right angle on the stone in order for it to sharpen, and guide rods can be purchased to help accomplish this. Pocket stones are available for taking into the field to keep the edge on the knife sharp and you should remember to wet the stone with water, often spit, or oil before sharpening begins.

Game or Net Bags

The net sportsman requires a moderate-sized bag which is comfortable to carry, preferably waterproof and capable of containing at least thirty pegged purse nets. The ferreter may choose a traditional game bag, a canvas fishing type bag, a home-made sack or a modern lightweight low-capacity rucksack.

I have paid as little as £2 and as much as £40 for net bags, but readily confess that the best deal was spotted by my brother who at the local agricultural show purchased a wax game bag for just over £10 that is large enough to take sixty nets and extremely comfortable to carry. If the bag is not waterproof simply place a plastic carrier bag in it as a liner in which to put the nets.

Wooden Mallet

I have found this to be an essential aid for setting nets correctly and recommend a mallet as part of the standard kit of every ferreter. I have rarely rabbited on ground which is soft enough for the net peg to be simply pushed into it even with the

Essential knife care equipment including different grade sharpening stones and oil.

A selection of suitable net-carrying bags ranging from the most expensive at the bottom to quite cheap ones on the top step.

full weight of the body behind it and have therefore found it best to place the peg in position and then give it a few firm taps with the mallet. A wooden mallet does not make much noise, is invaluable in frosty weather when the ground is frozen and makes certain the securing of the net. Alternatively, a small trowel could be used to open the ground up just enough to accept the lower two-thirds of the net peg.

Unnecessary or Optional Equipment

When my brother and I first got involved in ferreting we found a large number of items advertised as ferreting equipment which had the claim of being essential for the hunter. These ranged from archaic items that were commonly used earlier this century to sophisticated locating devices that have in recent years become very popular. However, much of what is advertised is either optional, not advisable for use or totally unnecessary. Mention is made in this section of items that remain in production and are available for purchase, despite recommendations against their use, so as to prevent the contemporary ferreter from being lulled into believing that they are compulsory purchases and then realizing at a later date that he will never use them. Consequently, this section is as much about what to avoid as what to buy.

Bells

Bells were used as a very primitive locator with the ringing of the bells supposedly helping to pinpoint the location of the ferret underground. They are of very limited value and very crudely suggest where the ferret might be. Furthermore, they hinder the ferret's natural predatory movement, alarmingly advertise its presence and get caught in the purse nets. Bells are of no value when hunting, but may be used when free exercising ferrets in the back garden or open spaces where they may wander or rush out of sight. The ringing of the bells will serve as an auditory reminder of the animals' presence and are useful for the purpose of keeping tabs on those ferrets inclined to roam.

Muzzles

Muzzles were used relatively commonly to prevent the ferret from killing the quarry below ground and at the time were the kindest option used by the ferreter, much kinder than resorting to clipping or filing the teeth. They, like bells, dull the sharpness of the animal's working abilities, prevent the ferret from protecting itself and reduce to nil its chances to survive should it inadvertently be lost whilst out hunting. For this reason many ferreters made their own muzzles out of string which would rot eventually or might include a slip knot which would free the ferret's jaws. However, by the time the string rotted, the ferret would already be in a poor condition. The question has to be asked, 'Are they necessary?' The answer is a definite no because if the ferreting procedure is carried out properly, the rabbits should be cleanly bolted and if they are not, a locator may be used to deal with any situation below ground.

A tool holder containing all the items needed to net a warren can be fitted onto the working ferreter's belt.

Mallets used to secure net pegs into hard ground.

Locators

Locators are invaluable pieces of equipment for those ferreters who dig regularly or who have ferrets that are prone to laying up. They cost around £50–60 for which the ferreter will acquire a transmitter that is fitted to a collar to be worn by the ferret below ground and a receiver that the keeper operates in sweeping arcs above ground. The receiver emits a bleeping or ticking noise that increases in volume and intensity as it is moved closer to the transmitter. It is contained within a light plastic box and an ear piece can be inserted for use when working in a spot where there are a lot of distracting sounds. The transmitter is fitted to a standard collar and should be placed over the ferret's throat to obtain the best results and minimize the possibility of getting caught as the animal works underground.

The locator enables the ferreter to pinpoint the exact position of his animal underground and eradicates the need for multiple digs. By so doing it means that a ferret that is laid or stopped up with a rabbit can be reasonably quickly retrieved and the quarry dispatched if it is still alive. For those who opt to dig when out rabbiting the locator is a compulsory labour- and time-saving tool and ferreters who use them cannot speak too highly about the devices.

Spades

Spades have been associated with ferreting for many years now and to some sportsmen for whom a good dig is akin to a successful day's working, they epitomize the ferreting endeavour. However, one does not have to dig to pursue rabbits with ferrets, although it is a skill at which all ferreters should be competent. It is only necessary to dig to retrieve a ferret that is laid up, to retrieve quarry killed below ground and to retrieve a ferret that cannot exit the warren of its own accord.

The skills required by the digger are the knowledge of the typical construction of a rabbit warren and its twisting tunnels, the ability to locate the right spot to dig either by traditional or modern locating methods and the confidence to dig without causing the warren to collapse.

The equipment needed for digging are a strong short-handled spade to cut out the turf and remove the top layer of soil, a long-handled spade to dig depth and a trowel to remove the final layer of soil. Kneepads or kneelers are also a good idea and are worth wearing for net setting as well as digging. With the exception of one expensive spade, all my digging tools have been acquired gratis either from skips or garden sheds where they are no longer wanted. The long spade that I had was discarded because it was too heavy to use, but for my purposes the weight is used to good effect to open up deep narrow holes in the ground. Therefore, I would suggest keeping your eyes open for a bargain as many of the old

A selection of spades including a long-handled spade, drainage spade, small rabbiting spade and on the left a triangular spade for delicate turf removal.

heavy spades are being left to rust and the owners would probably part with them for a small sum or even give them away. With a good clean up you will have an ideal rabbiting spade. The features that you should be looking for are a long handle and narrow blade.

It must be stated that it is by no means essential to dig in order to enjoy productive ferreting and I rarely if ever dig when out hunting. This is mainly because I served my ferreting apprenticeship on ground where the warrens were so close to hedgerows and trees that digging was not a sensible option due to the immense root systems just below the surface. Therefore, I had to rely on ferrets that would produce a clean bolt and continue to do so.

Ground-Clearance Equipment

Some of the warrens that the ferreter is often requested to work lie under dense undergrowth

Clearance equipment including a bill hook, pruning saw, large and small pruning shears, bushman's saw and a slasher or bush hook.

or are obstructed by branches of nearby trees and out-of-control hedging. In such cases permission is usually granted to remove the offending material so that the ferreter can net the entire warren and deploy his skills to good effect. All clearance work should be carried out prior to the day of the hunt – in fact, a week before the intended outing is ideal. The work itself should be done in a tidy fashion taking care to avoid any rare underlying flora. A typical list of clearance equipment would include a pruning and bushman's saw, large and small pruning shears, bush hook or slasher and a bill hook, many of which the enthusiastic gardener will already possess.

Clothing

Not only is ferreting a fieldsport that takes place during the coldest months of the year, but it requires its devotees to push and sometimes fight their way through natural obstacles and manoeuvre over barbed wire in order to get to the warrens. Consequently, the demands placed on the enduring ability of the ferreter's clothing are considerable and thought should be given to which garments will offer the best protection from the weather and piercing thorns and briers.

The choice of most ferreters is for waxed or thornproof clothing that keeps out the rain and will not tear on barbed wire or allow thorns to penetrate. A pair of leggings that fasten over a belt are worth wearing in dry as well as wet weather because they offer protection and more comfort when setting nets. Wellington boots are considered best for wet muddy conditions, but in cold weather or when I have got to walk long distances I much prefer well dubbined boots because they offer more support and are warmer. If the ferreter is hunting in wet weather and anticipates stopping for lunch during his outing, it is worth his while having two waxed jackets with one being used in the morning and the other in the afternoon. A waxed jacket takes some time to dry and one that is sodden is absolutely horrible to put back on again. A

comfortable hat should also be chosen to help maintain body heat in cold weather. The main features the ferreter should look for when choosing his protective wear are comfort based on being able to perform a full range of movements, and durability.

Vehicles

Nowadays most ferreters travel by road to the location where they intend to catch rabbits and they must possess a car that is capable of carrying all their equipment. Much of the farmland that I have gained access to is down long primitive tracks which play havoc with the treasured saloon car and many of the ferreters who use their family saloons park them further away from the actual working area, considering it wiser to walk extra distances than risk damaging the car. For this reason some choose to buy a cheap second car which is used only for ferreting.

The first ferreting car that I bought was an old Mini pickup, purchased from a farmer for £100, that proved to be a capable little country car, but 'little' was the operative word and my brother and I with a combined weight of thirty-two stones at the time craved for something a bit bigger. My dreams came true and I am now driving a Series 3 Land Rover which has the benefit of being suitable for daily use and ferreting without any risk of damage. Furthermore, it enables me to get right to the warrens themselves as some farmers are quite willing for me to take it over their land. The Land Rover acts in effect as a ferret shed on wheels due to the amount of equipment that I can transport in it and is obviously capable of going through the worst of conditions whilst providing a sense of security.

Making Your Own Equipment

Most ferreters are ardent adherents of the 'do-it-yourself' philosophy and extend the enjoy-

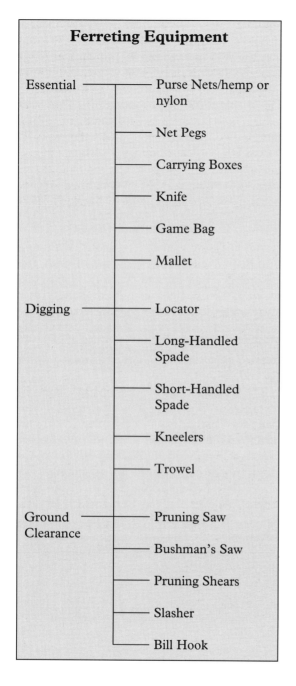

Ferreting Equipment

Essential
- Purse Nets/hemp or nylon
- Net Pegs
- Carrying Boxes
- Knife
- Game Bag
- Mallet

Digging
- Locator
- Long-Handled Spade
- Short-Handled Spade
- Kneelers
- Trowel

Ground Clearance
- Pruning Saw
- Bushman's Saw
- Pruning Shears
- Slasher
- Bill Hook

boxes, nets and net pegs and I will give a few general hints gained from my own experience that might prove helpful.

The making of a carrying box is no different from any other woodwork project and the same basic rules apply. The first thing to do is decide upon the size of the box and make a corresponding plan bearing in mind that the box is going to be carried long distances and should not therefore be too unwieldy. I make my carrying boxes out of exterior ply about half an inch thick because panel pins can be driven tidily through the corners to join the sides following a liberal application of wood glue. The other materials needed to complete the construction of a carrying box are two hinges, a clasp to fasten the lid and webbing to make the strap. My carrying boxes cost next to nothing to make due to a good supply of offcuts that I obtained for £5 from the timber yard; the best deals are always to be found at such yards. Remember that the carrying box is for animal transportation and therefore requires an adequate form of ventilation which can easily be achieved by the drilling of large holes approximating an inch in diameter.

Net pegs can also be made from exterior ply and painted to give them added strength and protection. I have cut a template of a peg out of cardboard and simply draw around it onto the wood when I require some new pegs. The net peg should be 6–8in long, $1\frac{1}{2}$in wide at the top tapering to 1in at the base. A hole should be drilled in the middle of the peg where it is broadest through which the drawcord of the net can be threaded.

Many of the older ferreters thought nothing of making their own purse nets for use in the field and the best bit of advice that I can offer concerning net making is to find yourself a good instructor. Making a net is really quite a simple task, but ambiguous instructions needlessly complicate the process and result in despairing toil and ridiculous looking nets. My first attempt at net making went drastically wrong due to the vague guidelines that were included in the so-called do-it-yourself kit that

ment of their pastime by making many of their own articles of equipment which, even if they do not look as good as commercially produced products, provide far more satisfaction. The most common home-made items are carrying

I had purchased. Even my father who has an engineering background was seen to scratch his head in bewilderment as he slowly worked his way through them and produced what may be loosely termed a net that I did not have the confidence to try in the field. Shortly afterwards I spotted a book by Howard G. Glynn entitled *Net-Making for Sport* and wondered whether it might be able to help us succeed in our arduous labours. When I received the book I was delighted to find clear instructions supported by pictorial aids and consequently set

about making my first net with renewed vigour – this time it was completed and successfully used when out hunting. Since then I have not looked back and now make all the additional nets that I need for my sport and quite enjoy the activity as a pastime in its own right. The equipment for making nets comprises a long plastic needle on which to load the nylon or hemp and a mesh measure. The materials include two steel rings, a length of spun nylon or polished hemp and a length of braided nylon for the drawcord and the actual making of the

Net-making equipment. From left to right: a spool of braided nylon, a loaded needle, wooden mesh measure, net under construction, rings, needle before loading, a spool of spun nylon.

net only really requires that you master one basic knot.

I have learnt to scrutinize nets much more carefully since I began to make my own and am a lot more knowledgeable about the features that collectively make a good purse net. Accessing the information to become a net maker is one of the best investments of time and money that I have made during my years as a ferreter and is one that I would heartily recommend to fellow sportsmen. If you do not have somebody to teach you the craft, the acquisition of the previously mentioned publication will put you well on the road to becoming an accomplished net maker.

8 THE FERRETING METHOD

Location

For the newcomer to the sport who purchased his working stock during the summer in anticipation of a long and fruitful rabbiting season, the beginning of September is joyfully received. However, there is more to successful ferreting than keen animals, a bag full of equipment and good intentions. Without access to quality land, all your hopes and expectations will be scuppered at the first hurdle.

Unlike the pre-1950s when vast numbers of rabbits were evident in every rural setting, the contemporary rabbit population as a whole is a lot sparser and is often located in pockets where numbers have recovered from the introduction of myxomatosis. Not only is good land upon which to ferret more difficult to find, but in a lot of cases the need for rabbit control is not required because of the feeling that myxomatosis is continuing to exert sufficient control on the rabbit. Furthermore, the heinous disease has made a martyr of the rabbit in the mind of many town and country dwellers alike who feel that the rabbit should be left alone due to its evil treatment in the past. During the last few decades a new movement has arisen that is protesting against the control of wild animals by means of fieldsports. The exponents of this movement have shown little concern for differentiating between the various forms of hunting, their values and any justifiable reasons for continuing their practice. Consequently, there is the voice and influence of anti-fieldsport sympathies to overcome.

Good land with dense populations of rabbits is coveted by sportsmen of various disciplines. Dog, gun, ferret and raptor are all used regularly to pursue the rabbit. Combined with a willingness to travel, in some cases a willingness to pay for the privilege and a lack of willingness to share rights, the difficulty in acquiring land can be considerable. On the other hand the opportunity to hunt on land where a rabbit is as difficult to find as a needle in a haystack has been offered to me with annoying regularity.

Anybody who has designs on enjoying good ferreting will require access to land that possesses certain characteristics. The features that he should be looking for are warren systems that can be netted and that appear to be in use. He will obviously desire ground that is heavily covered with rabbits and will be keeping an eye out for common signs of their presence. These include noticeable crop damage, diggings, rabbit droppings and fur as well as rabbits sitting out feeding at certain times. If rabbits are spotted, time should be taken to watch them, note their behaviour and record where they go to ground.

At various times I have been limited to hunting on ground that is unquestionably poor regarding its potential for the ferreter, and many novice rabbiters who have not had the opportunity to establish the contacts that more experienced hunters enjoy will ponder the validity of spending an entire day labouring in the field with ferret and net when only a single rabbit may be caught. However, one should not overlook the benefits of experience that can be gained from using poor land. You may not go home from such sites with a full bag, but the pride and joy of having ferrets that have

The rabbit is an alert animal with ears that can discern sounds from two different directions at the same time, eyes that have such a wide field of vision that they can virtually scan any direction and a nose that will detect any dangerous scents carried by the breeze.

managed to catch one or two rabbits on land and in warrens where the cards are stacked against them more than compensate for a smaller catch at the end of the day. Some of the best examples of working behaviour exhibited by both ferret and dog that I have experienced have occurred during those long and arduous days spent on ground that heavily favours the hunted. Consequently, I would heartily recommend that the ferreter continue to hunt on land that may be far from ideal and only yields a small bag.

When the keen ferreter is known in the local community, it is not uncommon for him to be offered rabbiting rights without having to canvass landowners. However, many sportsmen do not live in such small communities and may even have to travel some distance before finding land upon which to hunt. The first thing to be done when a good site is spotted is to ascertain who owns the land and on no account begin ferreting until permission is granted and any requirements of the owner understood and complied with. In our contemporary society wariness of strangers and concerns about theft of possessions and damage to property are considerable especially amongst those people who live in isolated positions and they will require reassurance before consent is given. After all, what would you do if following a knock on the door you opened it to find one or more probably two well-weathered men, who may not be easy to talk to and want permission to go in your back garden and catch crop damaging rabbits? Do you think you would let them in or would you be more likely to worry about the expensive equipment in the garden shed and the beautiful flower beds which have taken years and years to perfect? Considered like this, it is quite easy to understand why farmers and landowners are very cautious about who they let on their land.

My brother got far more rabbiting rights when he worked in the local community and the many farmers and landowners were able put a face to the name that they had heard associated with ferreting. If the enthusiastic hunter is not known personally to those from whom he seeks permission to hunt, he should endeavour to capitalize on his friendship with those people he knows well and who are on good terms with the farmers. In this way, at the very least, the ferreter will have gained for himself some credibility and get a fair hearing from the farmer he approaches. Sometimes we have not had the luxury of having a personal acquaintance as a go-between and have in such cases approached the relevant landowner directly in order to obtain permission to hunt. You will be able to ascertain the farmer's interest within the first couple of minutes by the kind of reception he extends to you. Make sure that the ferreting method is explained fully to him and it is a good idea to take along some of your animals to show him as their condition will reflect how seriously you take the sport and their tameness overcome many preconceived prejudices. Reactions are varied: some farmers will behave as if they are doing you a favour by allowing you to rabbit; some think you are doing them a favour; and others will not want you anywhere near their land for all the tea in China. When my brother was exchanging stories with a fellow ferreter who lived in the next county and bred a useful strain of polecats he

Common Signs of Rabbits

Crop damage including forestry.

Rabbit pellets.

Rabbit-runs through long grass.

Shallow random diggings.

Communal latrine.

Small amounts of fur.

Tracks in soft ground.

Warren.

Sightings of the rabbit and its most common predators.

could not believe his ears when the new acquaintance told him how the farmers in his locality actually paid the hunters in kind who went on their land and always gave them a little something special around Christmas time as a thankyou. We are always polite and endeavour to be professional when seeking permission to rabbit and respect the right of a landowner to decline our offer and will move readily on to pastures new.

Living in a small rural community we found ample opportunities to help people out and although our energies were spent without expecting any favours to be reciprocated we did benefit by being offered more and more rabbiting rights. There are also seasonal country jobs such as beating or potato picking which will help the ferreter get on the land and make useful contacts. At one time my brother and I were even asked to keep the pigeons off a field of newly sown oil seed rape in the farmer's absence and took to the task very seriously. When the farmer returned he arranged for my brother to go rabbiting, coursing and beating.

I would say that getting involved in country life is the best way to obtain access to good rabbiting land, but if this option does not for one reason or another suit you, you can try advertising in the local shops and newspapers as either a sportsman or pest controller. Keeping an eye on the local papers, especially the agricultural section can present you with some good opportunities. Last year I picked up our local paper and read with interest about a cemetery where the headstones were being undermined by the burrowing of rabbits. An enterprising ferreter quickly approached the parish council and secured for himself some very fine rabbiting. The moral obviously is to make the most of the opportunities as they arise. When the ferreter is granted permission, he should treat the trust bestowed upon him with due regard and endeavour to do a good job. We have been fortunate enough in the past to rabbit on golf courses, farms, large gardens and the splendid grounds of a public school.

The Day of the Hunt

My brother and I usually plan to arrive at the hunting site between 7 and 8am if this is agreeable to the landowners who have granted us permission. Our reason for selecting this time is because we are more likely to get numerous sightings of rabbits and at the beginning of the season it enables us to work the exposed warrens before the weather heats up and then to move on to the ones that are sheltered. If we were to start much before 7am during the winter months it would be much too dark to begin netting in earnest, especially when overcast. We adhere to the traditional season for ferreting that begins from mid-to late September and ends in March or early April.

Since it is primarily a winter sport, the ferreter has to endure the harshest of weathers if he is to enjoy regular excursions in the field although ferreters are divided in their opinion as to what are the best conditions in which to pursue the rabbit. My brother and I have ventured out in gusting winds, drenching downpours, hailstones and snow and have enjoyed success on every occasion. The actual effect of the weather on the process of ferreting is minimal and very much depends on how exposed are the warrens being worked. Sometimes we are able to work the exposed warrens of a bank in fine conditions and then move into the cover of a wooded rabbiting site, where there are ample natural shelters to shield us, should the weather take a sudden turn for the worse. The worse the weather is, the more likely are the rabbits to be in their underground sanctuary, the more difficult is the prospect of digging and the more reliant one becomes upon a ferret that knows its business and can produce a clean bolt time and again. The two fundamental considerations regarding weather conditions are the comfort of the ferreter and the comfort of his animals. With the advanced protective wear that is available today there is no reason why the well-prepared hunter cannot tolerate all weather conditions. As for the ferrets themselves, they experience minimal exposure to the weather because they are either in the carrying box or below ground. However, the dogs are a different matter altogether and wax jackets or a spell in the car should be considered for those canines which are not blessed with a dense weather-proof hairy coat. Nowadays most ferreters travel by road to ground where they can pursue the rabbit and all preparations and loading of the vehicle with equipment should have been undertaken before the day itself so that the ferreter can concentrate on the sport proper.

Deliberation on which or how many ferrets to take on the expedition will reflect knowledge of the size and perceived difficulty of the warrens to be worked. If the ferrets have been taken out during previous seasons the owner will have a good understanding of the strengths and weak-

nesses of his animals and be able to select those who work in a way which suits him best. Although my given preference is for working large polecat hobs, petite albino jills can be equally, and sometimes more, successful. Quite honestly take the ferret that you can handle in all situations and the one that you want to into the hunting field and pay little regard to those who say that only a certain type, size or gender will be competent. I have worked with large and small, young and old, polecat and albino ferrets and some in between and have been able to catch rabbits with all of them. Prior to the outing, I do not bother feeding the ferret because the feeding regime that I employ means that the animal is satisfactorily full from the last feed given. I always take a minimum of two

Loaded up for a day's working with everything that the ferrets, dog and I might need.

experienced working ferrets and usually four which are put into their straw-filled carrying boxes immediately before setting out.

When arriving at the intended location we will let the property owners know of our presence if they have previously required such notice, otherwise we will get straight down to work. Sometimes the farmers allow me to drive over their fields in my Land Rover which is the ultimate ferreting vehicle and acts as a portable ferret shed. It is always worth inquiring whether you can take a four-wheel-drive vehicle over the ground, but remember to drive it carefully so as not to leave damage in your tracks.

Net Setting

Throughout the course of its 700-year-old history people have managed to catch rabbits without the aid of locators or the arduous labours of prolonged digs which highlights the fact that ferreting is fundamentally concerned with the correct setting of nets combined with the deployment of ferrets and is the way in which I practise the sport today. Therefore, the emphasis of this working section is concentrated upon these two facets in particular while mention of more contemporary practices and the purpose of digging are included with some brevity in a later chapter.

The most common mistakes to be made when setting purse nets are to overlook exit or bolt holes connected to the warren, forget to secure the net pegs firmly and fail to entirely cover a hole with a net. Simple mistakes these may be, but when you are eager to catch the first rabbit of the day and experience the action of the hunt, the essential groundwork for success is important. Added to this there are the complications to net setting derived from the location of some warrens such as at the base of trees where the impenetrable root system obstructs the adequate placement of the net peg or there may be a gusting wind that keeps blowing the net away every time you set it. However, there are tricks of the trade that can be quickly learnt and make the setting of nets more interesting and enjoyable.

If you look carefully at the centre of the picture a rabbit run or trail can be seen and is one of the many signs of rabbit life that a ferreter should look for when surveying prospective hunting ground.

Before even unravelling the first net, the ferreter should take the time to have a good look at the warren. He will be looking at the size of the warren and check on the number of holes he and his marking dog can find. An appropriate number of nets will then be counted out and the process of net setting can begin in earnest. Different ferreters set their nets in slightly different ways with some being very meticulous and taking considerable time with each net while others seemingly throw the nets down in an instant. Some will have the same basic purse net for each and every hole and others have nets of varying lengths and shapes which are selec-

Although this may just look like a clump of grass to the casual onlooker, it is in fact a well-concealed bolt hole.

The bolt hole (above) uncovered.

tively used. All the nets that I have ever purchased were hand-made and now as a net maker myself I can actually design the nets keeping in mind the warrens that I work. If the ferreter has a good selection of nets, the shorter ones should be set over the simple holes such as the bolt hole and the extra mesh spaces provided by the longer nets used to good effect on awkward shaped and large holes.

After I have unravelled a net, I take hold of the rings in either hand, stretch the net to its full length and measure it up against the particular hole that I am concentrating on. Following this I lay the net down with one ring at the bottom and the other ring at the top of the hole and then drive the net peg into the ground about eight inches to a foot away from the top ring. I always secure my pegs by hitting them with a mallet and do this prior to anything else with the net because if I cannot find a good place for the peg the net will be useless anyway. Having satisfac-

torily secured the peg I take hold of the draw-cord just below the top ring and begin to pull the net open working my way down the cord to the bottom ring until the net is completely covering the hole. The bottom ring is then pushed slightly into the ground in the mouth of the hole. It is always worth standing back and surveying the net to make sure that it is maintaining its shape and remaining in position.

As I have mentioned, the ferreter comes across some warrens that present a problem from the netting point of view. When I first started to ferret in rural Cambridgeshire, I encountered difficult holes more often than I would have liked, but they did serve as a good apprenticeship and I did pick up a few useful tips that may help the reader. You must be prepared to compromise on your net setting sometimes even if it means possible escape for the odd rabbit or two. For example I have worked warrens where two holes have been dug

A set net should completely cover the hole and maintain its position.

close together in such a way that any attempt to net them separately would be useless and have therefore used my largest net to completely cover the opening created by the union of the two holes which will obviously give the second rabbit to bolt a chance to escape while I dispatch the first rabbit and reset the net.

I also had to work on a lot of steep banks where the top of the net collapsed every time I set it. If you encounter the same problem look on the ground for a thin twig or the hard stem of some nearby foliage and break off a couple of lengths approximately 1½in long. Insert these lengths into the square created by the mesh space that covers the ground near the top of the hole where the net keeps collapsing. They should only be pushed in gently so that they will hold the weight and help maintain the shape of the net. A good tug of the net or the force of a bolting rabbit hitting it should cause the lengths to fall and the net to purse concurrently.

One of the most beneficial items that the ferreter can take with him on a hunting expedition and which my brother insists on having is a ball of strong string for which he will find plenty of uses. My brother and I surveyed thoughtfully an inhabited warren which had bolt holes linked into the root system of a substantial beech tree and concluded that there was no possible way for us to push the net peg in. It was then that my brother reached for his renowned ball of string and set about placing a length of it around the

tree trunk as I watched doubtfully. Having tied a tight noose around the trunk he took a net and secured it by the drawcord to the noose and opened the net up over the bolt hole. About ten minutes elapsed before we were ready to enter the ferrets, but when they did go down a rabbit bolted into the net which pursed like a dream with the tree in effect acting as an anchor point and I had to applaud the ingenuity of my brother whose method I have copied since on many occasions with similar success.

For some ferreters the making and setting of nets is a pastime in its own right and it is vital that anyone going ferreting enjoys handling nets otherwise they will quickly get bored. Good net setting is fundamental to successful ferreting and the key to netting a warren well is to spend time on it and never rush the job.

A ferret can enter the warren through a set net without disturbing it. A careful look at this net will reveal that it is a double stranded one which I made out of hemp.

The ferret has resurfaced from the warren and is beginning to move through the net.

Entering the Ferret to a Netted Warren

A ferret that is taken rabbiting should be totally trustworthy and comfortable about being handled. It should also have had experience of being retrieved from pipes, artificial warrens and practice burrows and preferably be accompanied by a veteran worker if it is the animal's first outing. Do not venture forth into the field with a ferret that you are the least bit hesitant about handling or whose behaviour is unpredictable. Take time to handle and calm the ferret before entering it into the warren. This will enable the creature to settle its excitability at being released from the carrying box following a lengthy transit. Thus you make it aware of your presence in what is unfamiliar territory.

As the ferreter is busy netting up, he usually selects the hole into which he intends to enter the ferret. His decision will be guided by the fact that rabbits bolt uphill plus a good dose of intuition gained from years of hunting rabbits. Most books that I have read offer a counsel of perfec-

tion regarding where to enter the ferret and neglect to mention that it is not always easy to reach the ideal entry hole. Furthermore, if there is a particularly difficult or precariously netted hole, the ferret should be entered through that one as the rabbit will rarely bolt from the hole into which the ferret is entered. Most of my working ferrets have reached a stage of development now where they enter the warren of their own accord when placed upon the ground nearby and so are in the habit of choosing for themselves the best route of access.

Once the ferreter has set his nets there should be no reason to disturb them because the ferret, even if it is a large hob, should be able to go through the mesh spaces. The benefits of an animal that will move freely through the mesh spaces include ease, speed and the fact that the ferreter can watch from a distance as the animal exits one hole and enters another of its own volition.

Before entering the ferret, ensure that all the nets have remained in position – this is

My ferrets are used to exiting and entering the warren at their own discretion and are left alone to get on with their work while I watch from a safe distance.

especially important on windy days. As the ferret is entered it should be supported by both hands of the keeper so that it is not struggling to find secure footing. Always allow the ferret to see what it is doing by facing the head toward the net. Put the nose through the mesh and as the ferret moves forward, allow the animal to walk off your hand and enter the warren. Other ferreters choose to lift the corner of the net and place the ferret directly into the mouth of the hole before returning the net to its original position. Irrespective of which method is used, if the ferret protests at the choice of entry it should not be forced down, but gently stroked and calmed before trying again. If the animal continues to refuse, another entry point should be selected. As I have already mentioned some very experienced and capable hunting ferrets can be placed on the ground near a warren where nets have been set and they will find their own way without fuss or attention into the system.

Once the ferret has been entered, the keeper should take up a position where he can easily observe all the nets or, if he is working as part of a team, where he can cast a watchful eye over his allotted section. The ideal position is far enough away so that the ferreter is not visible to a bolting rabbit, but close enough to hear the thumping of the hind legs of the rabbit which means that it is on the move. On a clear day and in a situation located away from traffic, the thumping signal of the rabbit's hind legs can be easily heard and is a ready indicator of what is going on below ground. It is a sound that ferreters cherish and oftentimes they will lie prostrate on the ground with the ear inclined towards the warren in an effort to pinpoint the sound.

The virtue of patience must be exercised by the sportsman while his animal works the twisting underground tunnels of the rabbit warren. Ferreting is an unpredictable sport with variable amounts of time elapsing before the rabbits begin to bolt into the purse nets. The size of the warren will affect what the ferreter observes. It will not take a ferret long to work a small warren that consists of few chambers and the rabbit will be forced to bolt quite quickly. In a large warren the ferret will obviously have to hunt a great deal harder as the opportunities for evasion are far greater. This is the situation when entering two ferrets should be considered in order to close in upon the evasive rabbits. Without doubt the ferrets must be used to and enjoy one another's company to function effectively as a team. I have rarely worked warrens big enough to justify entering more than two ferrets at a time, but, have sufficient sociable stock at hand to enable me to do so if required.

As the rabbiter takes his ferrets out into the hunting field he will develop an understanding of the particular virtues possessed by each animal when working. I have some that operate like released cannons while others are painstakingly methodical and will leave no stone unturned in their pursuit of the rabbit. Some will be happy with a few rabbits bolting before resurfacing and others stubbornly refuse to exit the warren until each and every rabbit has left before it. It is the task of the keeper to assess the ground on which he intends to hunt and select those ferrets whose approach to their work best suits the warrens. The keeper must be prepared to give his ferrets time to do their work underground before rushing in with the spade which would hinder rather than help their efforts. Often he will see the face of the ferret appear at one of the bolt holes, turn around and disappear out of sight as it tracks down the rabbit and this is a good sign because if there were no rabbits in the warren the ferret would quickly exit and stop wasting its time below ground. The best indicator that I have of what is occurring beneath the surface is the reactions of the dogs with their sensitive hearing They will display controlled excitement and move towards the position from which the rabbits are about to bolt. If the dogs show no interest, I have learnt to trust their judgement and move on to the next warren.

The Catch

Finally, the moment the ferreter has been waiting for arrives and the rabbits begin to bolt one after another into carefully set purse nets and he must move quickly and efficiently in order to dispatch the animals humanely. Before the hunter reaches this point, he should have carefully thought about the reality of killing rabbits with his hands and reconciled himself to the task. Unlike shooting where the projectile does the work for the hunter, the ferreter will be required to use his physical force to dislocate the neck of the rabbit and will feel its life ebbing away. Just because a person is raised or interested in the countryside does not mean that he will be proficient at killing animals and he may lack the incentive or the technique for the task. Consequently, it is something that I gave considerable thought to before I started rabbiting. Could I kill the rabbit and could I do it properly? At first I was actually relieved when the rabbits got away or the terrier beat me to the deed, but when four rabbits bolted all at the same time I was forced to act and did so automatically. I delivered a chop to the base of the skull and passed the rabbit to my brother who confirmed that the animal was dead much to my relief. Since then I have killed many rabbits quickly and humanely which remains my prime objective and recommend that the beginner who is new to the sport learn this job from a more experienced hand.

Which Technique?

I favour the use of a sharp blow to the base of the rabbit's skull which breaks the neck causing instantaneous death. The only downside to this technique is that it can cause trauma to the area that is hit resulting in some localized bleeding. This may make the carcass unsightly which may be a problem if the intention is to sell it. I prefer the chop method because it is quick and easy, can be carried out while the rabbit is still in the net, requires little skill and rarely fails.

The other technique used is the dislocation method similar to that used on chickens and the commercial success of humane dispatchers of poultry and game is testimony to the fact that many people cannot master this technique. Therefore, it should be taught by a knowledgeable countryman rather than learnt by experience. My brother is adept at both methods, but favours the chop for the reasons mentioned and believes there to be a greater chance of failure when dislocation is performed by inexperienced hands.

The Chop in Action

When the rabbit bolts into the net and is tidily pursed, pick it up with one hand around the loins and hold it still about the level of the waist. Immediately you should strike the rabbit at the base of the skull with the edge of the other hand in a downwards movement towards your feet. One blow of reasonable force should prove sufficient to kill the animal and prevent unnecessary suffering.

Having successfully killed the rabbit, the ferreter has to deal with the carcass which includes peeing, legging, skinning, paunching and jointing.

Peeing or Thumbing

It is a good idea to empty the rabbit's bladder immediately after killing it as this will prevent the contents being released if the bladder is pierced with a knife when skinning. Peeing is a simple matter of holding the rabbit by its front legs with one hand, placing the other hand firmly around the abdomen with the thumb in line with the base of the rib cage and moving the thumb down towards the tail in a straight line and maintaining a constant pressure. If there is a steady trickle of urine as the thumb moves towards the tail the task has been done correctly and the rabbit's bladder will be empty.

Legging

As soon as peeing is completed the rabbit should be hung by the hind legs so that all the blood drains to the head which will pale the flesh and for some reason makes skinning a lot easier. To hang a rabbit a slit is made approximately 4cm long between the major bone, or femur, of one hind leg and the tendon which lies directly behind it. To locate the correct position, take hold of a hind leg to find the elbow joint or hock and look immediately above it to where there is a long narrow depression of skin through which a knife will easily cut. Having made a cut, the foot of the other hind leg is inserted through the opening up to the hock and the rabbit will then be able to hang on a nearby branch. Legging also makes the task of carrying the rabbits easier as two carcasses can be joined by interlocking the hind legs before draping them over shoulder, stick or spade.

Skinning

After a successful day in the field I take my weary body home and am faced with another list of tasks to perform before the day is complete and I can indulge in rest. One of the most obvious of these is the skinning of the rabbit for which a clean area, sharp knife, meat cleaver and two buckets are needed. Some people tie the rabbit to a hook or nail while others are happy to hold the carcass whilst skinning. There are two common methods for skinning which are outlined below.

Method 1
   a) Place the point of the knife just beneath the skin at the point of the hock on one hind leg.
   b) Cut down the leg in a straight line across the top of the vent and up the other hind leg until the hock is reached.
   c) Cut away the tail.
   d) Peel the skin off the hind legs and pull down the body until the front legs are reached.
   e) Free the front legs and when the neck is reached, chop it off with the meat cleaver taking care to avoid your fingers.

Method 2
   a) Chop off the back paws at the hock joint and the front legs at the knee joint.
   b) Place the tip of the knife beneath the rabbit's skin at a point between its hind legs.
   c) Run a cut up to the back of the rib cage.
   d) Peel back the skin over the rabbit's flanks with the fingers until a gap between the backbone and skin appears.
   e) Manipulate the hind legs until they can be pulled through the skin.
   f) Cut off the tail.
   g) Draw the skin down the front third of the body over the forepaws and up around the neck.
   h) Take the meat cleaver and chop off the head. Use one bucket to place waste in and one for rinsing the hands and cutting tools as they become bloodied.

Paunching

Paunching is the removal of the guts and is a simple matter of making a small incision in the stomach and pulling the flesh open with the fingers all the way up to the rib cage. The paunch or guts will now fall forward through the opening and can be pulled free of its join with the liver and dumped in the waste bucket. Organs such as the kidneys, liver and gall bladder will now be apparent and can be easily removed by hand. At the bottom of the rib cage, the diaphragm is located and with gentle sustained pressure this muscle which separates the stomach from the chest can be penetrated and the heart and lungs pulled out. I give the liver, heart, kidneys, lungs and head to my ferrets, but dispose of the intestines. The final job of paunching is to cut away a small piece of cut overlying the pelvis, following which the rabbit is ready to be jointed. Experienced countrymen and women can paunch and skin a rabbit in a matter of minutes and the ferreter must be prepared to practise his technique in order to become proficient.

Jointing

Rabbits can be cooked whole, but many recipes require the rabbit to be jointed which means separating the fore and hind legs from the body and cutting the body in half. Because people are going to eat the flesh, it is important that a tidy job is made, although my first efforts looked very ropey. The process is as follows:

   a) Cut off the loose skin on the flanks.
   b) Remove the hind legs by performing a 360 degree cut around the natural contour at the top of each hind leg that penetrates to the bone. Then simply pop the leg out of the hip joint.
   c) Remove the forelimbs in similar fashion.
   d) Divide the body at the midsection by striking the bone with a meat cleaver. At the conclusion of jointing you should have two flaps, four limbs and two body portions and the rabbit is now ready for storing or cooking.

Cooking

My mother continues the tradition of fine country cooking using homegrown produce and indigenous quarry and the recipes below include those which I have enjoyed following a days rabbiting.

Cottagers Traditional Rabbit Pie
   Two jointed rabbits
   4oz bacon
   Water
   Potatoes
   8oz shortcrust pastry

Place the joints of rabbit in a pan with bacon that has been cut into shreds. Add seasoning and cover with water. Simmer gently for 1–1½ hours until the meat is tender. Peel some large potatoes and place a layer of them sliced over the base of a pie dish. Turn the rabbit with all the gravy into the pie dish. Put more sliced potato over the rabbit and lastly cover with pastry. Decorate and cut a hole in the top before putting into a hot oven for 45 min. This will make a delicious meal for eight.

Rabbit Casserole
    Two rabbits
    1 cup of fresh breadcrumbs
    4 large onions
    1lb bacon
    Sweet marjoram and sage
    Salt and pepper

Soak the rabbit joints in salt water overnight and then roll them in flour and place in the casserole dish. Mix the breadcrumbs with seasonings to taste. Moisten with a little milk and sprinkle among the rabbit pieces. Slice the onions over the top and cover it all with boiling water. Cut the bacon into thin strips and lay on the top. Cover the casserole and bake in a moderate oven for $1\frac{1}{4}$ hours. Take the lid off and brown the top and serve steaming hot with vegetables. This traditional northern meal will also serve 8.

Rabbit with Tomatoes
    One jointed rabbit
    1oz butter
    4oz belly of pork
    Garlic, crushed
    Two sliced onions
    1tsp Basil
    15oz tinned or fresh tomatoes
    1tsp tomato purée
    1tsp sugar
    Salt and pepper

Melt the butter in a flame-proof casserole dish. Gently brown the pork and rabbit joints. Add the crushed garlic, onions, basil and tomatoes. Simmer for 10 min. Stir in the purée and sugar. Season with salt and pepper. Cover and cook in the oven for $1\frac{1}{2}$ hours. Serve with boiled rice. Serves 4.

9 DOGS FOR FERRETING

Realizing the Value of a Rabbiting Dog

The acquisition of his first ferret, a large albino hob with an amiable disposition and boundless zeal for working, inspired realistic hopes in my brother's mind of large bags and fast-paced sport. However, despite his diligent efforts and arduous toil in setting nets and deploying the ferret, he regularly returned home after a day's hunting with nothing to show for his labours – just an empty bag, a downcast expression and an emerging bald spot where he had incredulously rubbed his head in obvious surprise that he never caught anything even though his hob entered the rabbit warren with purpose and determination. He knew there was an abundance of rabbits in that part of the country – a fact that was verified by the farmers' incessant bitter complaints about crop damage and his own numerous sightings when out walking; this only added insult to the injury of his failure in the hunting field. Not suprisingly he began to think that the rabbits were equipped with an advanced early-warning system that enabled them to detect the approach of the ferret before arrival so that they could vacate the warren and watch with hilarity from afar. Even the hob showed signs of being brassed off and looked at my brother imploringly, willing him to do something that would change the tide of their misfortune. But, what could my brother, John, do? He had followed the guidance of books, old and new, to the letter and still came up with nothing. Then when it seemed that he was condemned to be the ferreter who never caught a rabbit, a stroke of good fortune led to a chance meeting with Stan, an elderly ferreter who never returned home without a rabbit or two to show for his labours.

Stan was a man of colossal proportions who carefully rationed his words and had seemingly little use for smiling. John met him one crisp October morning as he was returning home from a long walk with our boxer dogs which one of Stan's trio of terriers attempted suicidally and in vain to attack. Fortunately, my brother managed to retrieve the boxers before they took aversion to the pathetic taunts of the terrier for which Stan was courteously, but economically apologetic before continuing his journey. Upon seeing a sturdy box hanging from Stan's shoulders John, keen to observe and learn from this man, hastily asked,

'Can I go ferreting with you?'

Stan simply shook his head and was about to continue on his way when the trilby-clad head of the nearby farmer came into view. He had been brought from the barn by the incessant barking of the aberrant terrier.

'Come on Stan, let the lad go with you,' the farmer interceded.

Stan thought for a few moments and then relented, but he was not going to wait about all day and my brother had to get rid of the boxers posthaste. John ascertained the direction in which Stan intended to go and knowing the land well promised to join him within ten minutes which prompted a doubtful smirk across the elderly ferreter's face. He obviously believed that my brother would not make it home with the dogs and back again within the time and therefore he would be released from the tedium of company during his days sport. But without delay John trotted up to a surprised Stan who began to show some affection in response to the enthusiasm of his younger companion and gave a wry smile when my brother divulged details of his regular cross-country running that enabled him to cover the ground so quickly.

Stan was going to work ground that John had hunted on numerous occasions previously with absolutely no success, yet the elderly man possessed such a degree of assurance that a watcher would have believed the rabbits to be already in the bag. Stan had three dogs, a Jack Russell derivative, an elderly Norwich and a deviant Patterdale. In businesslike fashion each dog went off in a different direction with the little Jack Russell routing slowly through the long grass while the Norwich ambled about in a field of sprouts and the Patterdale thundered through thorn bushes and dived in ditches with seeming reckless abandon. Within a very short period of time terrified rabbits appeared and fled frantically for the security and protection of the burrow fearing for their lives. Any rabbit that decided stupidly to try and hide out quietly above ground soon found itself in the determined grip of one of the tenacious terriers. Several rabbits were accounted for in this manner and the ferrets were not even out of the box yet!

Stan then proceeded to give my brother a vital lesson regarding rabbit habits of which the hunter needed to be aware. He told him that the indigenous rabbits in that part of the country were what is known as surface rabbits, choosing like their relative, the hare, to live above ground in an attempt to combat the dreaded myxomatosis that spreads like wildfire underground. At last, my brother had the answer to his unproductive and woeful ferreting expeditions – quite simply that the rabbits did not live in the burrows, but only used them for protection or breeding.

The first warren that was netted yielded up a brace of good-sized rabbits that had been chased down by the marauding dogs. The speed with which the rabbits readily bolted was a surprise to my brother who believed, as stated

---

Dogs for Rabbiting

Most popular:

> Jack Russell Terrier
>
> Patterdale
>
> Whippet
>
> Lurcher

Less commonly used:

> Cairn Terriers
>
> Border Terriers
>
> Norfolk Terriers
>
> Heelers
>
> Beagles
>
> Bassets
>
> Dachshunds
>
> Border Collies

---

in many books, that a rabbit aware of a canine hunter above ground will not bolt from the warren. Stan matter of factly stated that with a ferret up its backside, a rabbit is going to shift forgetting all about the dogs that have just chased it. He reinforced his hypothesis time and again as rabbits which had been purposefully chased underground bolted from burrow after burrow.

Despite the hasty and ill-advised attack on the boxers, John thought that in accordance with sporting literature the terriers would manifest behaviour that was quiet, calm and patient when working, but his expectations were misplaced. Stan's most successful hunting dog was a frenetic Patterdale that made my brother feel dizzy with its frenzied comings and goings. The deviant never stopped barking all morning and yet still managed to account for four out of the ten rabbits in the bag by midday and that number was soon to rise as it dashed down a fallen tree trunk until it got itself well and truly stuck. Stan heaved and pulled the animal's back legs with all his might in an effort to extricate it and eventually after much tugging and twisting that seemed enough to tear the dog in two it popped out like a cork from a champagne bottle with a rabbit tightly gripped between its teeth. Despite the manic behaviour of the Patterdale, it was obvious that his success and determination made him a firm favourite with his sporting

Basic obedience is vital for a working dog. Here my brother's Jack Russell shows the sit position.

master who had perfected the talent of getting the best from his dog.

Suitable Breeds

My brother enjoyed his day with Stan and learnt that the dog has a valued role to perform on behalf of the ferreter. He set his sights firmly on acquiring for himself a rabbiting canine and started to scrutinize the suitable breeds and select the one that suited him best. The Jack Russell terrier, whippet and lurcher are the most commonly and successfully used dogs associated with the practice of ferreting and all the authoritative works on the subject of rabbiting will highlight the abilities and recommend the purchase of these dogs.

The Jack Russell Terrier

No right-thinking ferreter would refuse the company of one of these spirited little canines that epitomize in every fibre of their being the characteristics of a dog designed for rabbiting. Initially bred by their human namesake for accompanying the horse and hound in pursuit of fox, the Jack Russell failed to establish a unified standard that was acceptable to the registry of the Kennel Club of Great Britain. The dogs varied in size, with the early terriers of the Parson's breeding measuring approximately 14in at the withers, while others that shared a similar appearance and conformation were as short as 9in at the withers. Consequently, the Jack Russell was until recently a type of terrier rather than a definite breed and was easily recognized by the public as a homogenous title

The Patterdale is a traditional and well-proven rabbiting dog.

for both long- and short-legged varieties. As I viewed the terrier group at Crufts last year I was particularly impressed with the smart appearance of the Parson's Jack Russell terrier, but hope to see the continuance of breeding of those so-called Jack Russells that fail to comply with the breed standard and are perpetuated because of their working qualities which is of primary importance to me as a sportsman and I must confess that all the ferreting Russells I have encountered are too short to enter the show ring.

The Jack Russell type, as we shall call it, can be smooth or broken coated and measure anything from 9in–13in. They are obviously not bred from a line of pure-blood Parson's, but in my experience make the best ratting and rabbiting terriers. Their longer-legged relatives are favoured by the hunt who view their sole purpose in life as working to fox and therefore they have not had the opportunity to try their talents at rabbiting in the belief that it would distract them from their primary function. In my opinion, however, one of the greatest displays of instinctive and creative hunting behaviour is to be seen when a Jack Russell accompanies ferrets on a day's rabbiting.

I can certainly bear witness to the merit of my brother's Russell bitch who with a height of 11in at the shoulder weighs in at a hefty 13lb and possesses lightning reactions that have accounted for the demise of a number of rabbits that would otherwise have escaped. On one of her first outings she leapt into the small hollow of a fallen tree to emerge with the first catch of the day. Then, while working a bank that same morning and after having had six rabbits bolt obligingly into our nets we began to gather up our equipment and turn our attention to the next warren when she suddenly darted into the burrow up to her back legs and immediately began to reverse to reveal a rabbit that had thought it had got away in her mouth.

The size of the bitch is her blessing because she can squirm in virtually anywhere either to flush out an idling rabbit or guard an exit hole that cannot be adequately netted. She will eagerly go through briar and bracken whether there be wind, rain or hail in her relentless pursuit of the rabbit and irrefutably enjoys every minute of her working day. The Jack Russell type is tenacious, lively, full of character and ideally suited to the country dweller in general and the rabbiter in particular.

The Patterdale
Amongst sportsmen the Patterdale is as able as the Jack Russell when it comes to rabbiting. Bred to work in the rugged and rocky terrain of the fells, the Patterdale is a hardy, sure-footed and active animal. They were bred for the gameness needed to face the hill foxes that they encountered in the extremely cold weather conditions experienced at 2,000ft above sea level. They have a hard dense coat that is wiry and quite weather resistant and weigh between 14 and 16lb. Coat colour varies from black to blue and includes liver, red and black and tan.

The Patterdale is a courageous, intelligent and obdurate little animal which has proved time and again to be an effective pot filler for the ferreter. My brother appears to suffer from what is best described as Patterphobia because he dislikes them and every Patterdale he meets tries to bite him, but he readily admits that the best rabbiter he ever met was a Patterdale called George. The Patterdale requires firm discipline to curb its enthusiastic and sometimes reckless behaviour, but is well worth the effort.

Other Terriers
From West Highland Whites to Norwiches, Yorkshires to Cairns, Borders to Norfolks, all possess the essential abilities to be rabbiting dogs if trained and encouraged from an early age. Terriers are by nature tenacious and instinctive animals which if given half a chance will prove themselves useful and it would be a brave person to claim that a terrier is bereft of working ability, merely because it has been bred to a uniform standard. However, establishment as a registered breed and increasing popularity as pets has seen the cost of such terriers reach

substantially higher prices than Patterdales and the Jack Russell type. Understandably, most fieldsportsmen are unwilling to pay for pedigree terriers which are not from proven working stock when for a fraction of the price keen rabbiting Russells and Patterdales can be easily acquired.

The main difficulty encountered when training a terrier of any breed or type to rabbit is the control of the extreme excitability that the quarry enlivens in the canine. It is generally accepted amongst terrier enthusiasts that the hunting of rabbits with such dogs is more difficult for the keeper than the pursuit of fox and most huntsmen maintain the view that their terriers will have their purpose thrown into ruination if they are allowed to pursue rabbits. This is because they will not remain steady when hunting fox and choose the scent of any rabbit which they encounter. Consequently, the terrier, despite its history of facing larger quarry, is an animal that seems naturally to favour hunting smaller quarry such as the rabbit. Because of this inherent enthusiasm and the tenacious character of the terrier, the owner should initiate a thorough and well-disciplined training programme in order for the dog to use its abilities in compliance with its master's wishes. A terrier that is well trained cannot be beaten as a rabbiter and it could be rationally suggested that every ferreter should have at his heels one of these spirited little animals. Mayhew, Sewell and Cousens, writing about dogs during the last century, echo this sentiment in the following words, 'No Englishman should be without a terrier; they are the salt of life and on occasion even the whole cruet, including the oil. Provided you have taught your terrier to be obedient, not with the whip, but with inflexible firmness and patience, beginning as soon as he starts to run about, and, after his obedience is obtained, leave him in possession of his confidence and individuality, he will learn his work quickly and well, and will be a delight to his owner and a continual happiness to himself.'

The Whippet

Apart from terriers the most commonly used dog for ferreting is probably the Whippet which has proved itself to be an excellent rabbiting dog due to its tremendous speed of acceleration combined with a willingness to hunt both open and covered areas. To behold these animals in full motion is quite breathtaking and corrects the common misconception that their appearance denotes fragility as every muscle and sinew of the body bespeaks their design for speed. The rabbit suits the Whippet as quarry because it too shares a sharp acceleration and is therefore a challenge; however, it is not too large a burden for the dog to comfortably manage.

The Whippet, considered to be the poor mans Greyhound, is commonly thought to have emerged as a breed in the mid to late nineteenth century and was the product of interbreeding Greyhounds, Manchester Terriers, Bedlington Terriers, Italian Greyhounds and the now extinct English White Terrier. Many modern rabbiters believe the Whippet capable of working undergrowth and hedgerows in similar fashion to the terrier as well as having the keenness of eye and fortune of speed to close in upon a rabbit in the open. Consequently, this diminutive sighthound combines the talents of both Greyhounds and Terriers to make it a first-rate ferreter's dog and successful pot filler.

The Whippet has a short, smooth coat which requires no trouble and is capable of enduring the worst of weathers and harshest of conditions when working. The coat may be had in a variety of colours such as black, red, white, brindle, fawn, blue or mixtures of them. Approximately 17–19in the Whippet weighs in either side of the 20lb mark depending upon its gender.

The familiar features of a Whippet are a long lean head, deep and roomy chest, broad square back which is rather long and slightly arched over the loins, long forelegs, strong hindquarters, well-bent stifles, round feet and a long tapering tail, all of which denote the obvious build for speed. As for the temperament of the Whippet, it is considered to be a gentle, calm and affectionate companion with a trainable and amenable nature which makes it a pleasure to own.

The lurcher, generally with Whippet antecedents, has become increasingly popular within both the pet and working world and is proving itself useful. However, it possesses no advantages over a good working Whippet which proves to be just as hardy as these selective hybrids and faster over ground. Obviously, the entire list of longdogs and lurchers are capable of being used to catch rabbits, but none is more suited to this task than that traditional companion of the northern working man, the Whippet.

Unusual Rabbiting Dogs

Unfortunately, many contemporary pedigree breeds fail to be used for purposes that suit their breeding and challenge their instincts. Consequently, the working capability of such animals is obscured and opportunities for them to show their talents lessened. Such a situation has awakened a desire within me to give dogs with a fine sporting heritage and a pedigree the chance to experience the sport of ferreting. The unusual rabbiting dogs listed in this section include those that I hope to trial in the future and are worth considering by the more eccentric ferreter.

The Basset

The Basset is a substantial hound set upon short legs that possesses a mild and steadfast nature. This breed of dog first came to the shores of Britain in the middle of the nineteenth century and towards the end of that same century began to be used for the hunting of hares. The shortness of the hound is one of the dog's many

These Griffon Bassets have amazing scenting ability and are reputed to be wonderful hedge dogs. They have been used to good effect in France by Comte Elie de Vézins in pursuit of hare.

virtues because at a height of 13–15in it is able to work its way through thorn and scrub that would prove impenetrable to larger dogs. Furthermore, the Basset has a nose which will not bypass any quarry and remains staunchly on the scent until the hunt is over. The Basset is not a limited hunter, but can use its abilities to pursue a range of quarry including hares, pheasants and rabbits for which it is used with some regularity in the United States. It is a dog that willingly works all terrains and with such a great aptitude for hunting should be of some use to the ferreter and I would certainly like to have one for working the hedgerows. The only problems are the relatively high price of purchase and the tendency to give voice, that apparently is a lovely bell-like melody. I do not believe giving voice to be too great a problem to overcome

and despite what others have said have seen rabbits bolt time and again when the dogs have been making a tremendous noise above ground.

The Dachshund

The Dachshund was bred in Germany for the purpose of dealing with the indigenous badgers. The Dachshund is a small dog weighing around 20lb and may have a short, long or wire-haired coat. It is an intelligent and persevering animal and a miniature version weighing between 9 and 11lb was bred specifically by German sportsmen during the latter half of the nineteenth century for going to ground after rabbits. They belong to the meritorious army of workers and are really dual-purpose dogs because they will go to ground like terriers or track wounded game on the surface.

The Russell in the stay position from which she will not stir until commanded. This is vital when setting the dog in a position to guard the hole.

Other Breeds

Living in a rural community, I have had the opportunity to meet people who own various types of dogs that have encountered rabbits. One woman who had bred working dogs for many years and previously kept terriers claimed that her line of miniature poodles were the best little rabbiters she had ever seen.

A common sight where I live is the farm dog of Border Collie origin and my brother when he worked on a dairy farm that had such a dog remembers how it would daily return from the fields with a rabbit in its mouth. Clearly, dogs are not willing to confine themselves to our misconceptions about what they should and should not be able to do. Therefore, if the ferreter desires a dog other than a terrier or lurcher, there is no reason why it should not accompany him when rabbiting and there is a great deal of satisfaction to be gained from training such a dog to be useful. For those who

nod their heads in incredulity at the thought of dogs other than the traditional working breeds being of use to the ferreter I would like to offer this next section that concerns my very unusual country dog.

The Mongrel

I remember well the days when my brother would return home from work and announce with glee that he had acquired yet more rabbiting rights and in addition obtained permission for the dogs to accompany us, having assured the landowners that they were working canines. This was all very well for him with his archetypal Jack Russell bitch who looked the part for rabbiting and ratting, but my idiosyncratic mongrel was hardly what people were expecting from a serious fieldsportsman and I was constantly on the defensive should any derogatory remarks be forthcoming.

What kind of ferreter acquires a mongrel? one

My mongrel bitch was bred for no purpose, but is useful when rabbiting and is an excellent all-round country dog.

may justly ask. The answer is, I am afraid, a sentimental one who had grown impatient with unfulfilled promises made by an aristocratic lurcher enthusiast and who was made aware of a puppy, eight weeks of age, in need of care and attention. Throughout history the exploits of countrymen, whether herdsmen, shepherds or hunters, have testified to the value of the trained working dog. One such beneficiary is the ferreter for whom a suitable dog will help to locate the intended quarry, send it below ground and catch it above ground as well as guard holes that cannot be netted. My brother's Russell bitch was an obvious choice as a rabbiting dog and justified her credentials time and again in the field. Consequently, my brother could hold his head up high and constantly relate the adventures of his tailor-made broken-coated bundle of mischief.

The mongrel on the other hand is a non-conformist, without type and standard, of widely varying descent and bred for neither work nor show ring, but some books do suggest that the cottagers favoured large mongrels which makes one wonder whether this animal of lowly birth has something to offer the countryman. Scratching the surface of the canine world would suggest not. Mongrels are sold for next to nothing or are given away, are the most frequent visitors to animal sanctuaries and the most commonly abused canines. However, throughout its history the mongrel has shown adaptability and overcome prejudice by succeeding in pursuits that have been considered the reserve of pure or hybrid animals.

The mongrel is bred for no working purpose and therefore generally has few expectations placed upon it, so there was no indication of how my bitch, Sally, would respond to my endeavours to shape her into the country dog I desired. My requirements were that she should be sociable with people and dogs, broken to livestock, unhesitatingly obedient to command and willing to accompany me no matter what task I was performing in the country. My early optimism was not misguided. House and basic obedience were soon realized and my mother,

who had trained Boxer dogs some years before, affirmed that Sally had the potential to achieve much, dependent upon the extent to which I was willing to train her. It is eight years now since I began with Sally and I must confess that she has far exceeded my expectations both as a companion and accomplice when working in the field.

She does not and never will have the sheer hunting instincts of a terrier or the speed of a Whippet, but she will use her nose to mark with the same accuracy as the terrier and I have learnt to disregard a warren if she does not reckon on it. Sally is used to giving chase to any escapees or rabbits residing above ground and will remain at the warren where they have found refuge. On the odd occasion, she has been able to turn the rabbit into the path of my brother's Russell who will effortlessly dispatch it, and both dogs are used successfully to patrol those holes that we are unable to set. She also possesses the fitness to endure a day's working in all weathers, is calm enough to wait quietly once the ferrets are entered and responds quickly and appropriately once the action begins.

A countryman should never leave the house without a good hat on his head and a good dog by his side and I for one feel incomplete whether I am out felling trees, gleaning fruit from the hedgerows or digging the vegetable plot if I cannot see Sally lying nearby. Accompanying me in such activities means that she must be trustworthy with sheep, cattle, wildfowl, poultry and of course ferrets and she has been broken to horses and pigs with the greatest of ease. Her amenable and sociable nature has won her many admirers from young children to old ladies and has helped to build a reliable reputation among the landowners from whom we seek rabbiting rights.

Sally has become involved in a host of country pursuits from herding sheep to lifting pheasants, at which, according to my brother who wrote on beating some years ago for the *Shooting Times*, she excels and can compete with gundogs. I can honestly say that she enthusiastically attempts all that I ask of her and has consequently proven that a mongrel can make a purposeful and pleasing working dog. But there are limits to her abilities and she does not exhibit the same excellence in the field when out ferreting as those bred for the purpose. However, I have never witnessed such an effortless training of a dog to livestock as that which I enjoyed with Sally. On those rare occasions when I dream of the future and of catching rabbits in particular I envisage having a Whippet or terrier and believe that I will be able to train the animal better because of my experiences with my unusual, but by no means useless country dog.

Conclusion to Breeds

There is no shortage of options for the ferreter to choose from regarding a suitable and capable dog that can be used when rabbiting. Those with either limited experience of hunting or of dog training would be well advised to select from the traditional and proven working breeds that will educate the keeper as much as the keeper will teach the dog. The more knowledgeable trainers may wish to take up the challenge of a more obscure breed that may not have actively been involved in rabbiting for some generations. Whatever the choice of the keeper, it goes without saying that a well-trained dog will prove a benefit and pleasure to the owner.

Training

Having secured himself a sound specimen, most probably from that mischievous clan of terriers or the aristocratic-looking Whippets, the keeper is faced with the decision of how best to train the animal. As a prelude it is worth stating that training should be an experience of mutual enjoyment for both man and dog, should be conducted in a patient and controlled manner, and built upon a relationship of appropriate affection with the dog. The more obedient the ferreter's dog is, the more useful it is, the more

agreeable is its companionship and the happier also is the animal itself.

For our purposes training may be divided into three distinct areas which are:
1. Basic obedience.
2. Advanced obedience.
3. The encouragement of natural instincts.

Basic Obedience
A programme of basic obedience training should begin in earnest when the puppy has reached an age of between four to six months, irrespective of breed, and is able to display a degree of concentration. During this period the keeper will teach his dog to obey the following commands:

1. Come here!
2. Sit down!
3. Heel!
4. Stay!
5. Lie down!

I will not go through the actual mechanics of teaching and reinforcing these commands as there are many good books on the market devoted to the subject of dog obedience in great depth, but I do hope to highlight the validity to the ferreter of each movement. In order for the training to be effective it is worth bearing the following in mind:

1. Always verbalize each command in the same manner, as variations, no matter how small, may cause confusion and undue stress for a willing dog. If you have taught the dog to obey the command, 'Sit down, Sally!' on one occasion, you should not then change it to merely 'Sit!' on another. All commands must be crisply delivered, short and consistent.
2. Training sessions should be kept reasonably short and made enjoyable. Five to fifteen minutes, 2–3 times a day will prove sufficient. There is no benefit to be gained from overtiring or boring a compliant animal.

3. Refrain from using force and punishing the dog which will break its confidence and injure its soul. Discipline should be achieved by the tone of voice, stance and gestures of the owner.

Come here!

The ferreter's dog should return to its master on request in order to be redirected to a different area to work or to avoid possible danger. When out ferreting if my dog did not heed my command to come, she might have rushed into electric fencing or remained in a position that hindered a successful bolt, to name but a few of the problems that could have occurred.

Sit down!

This command is needed to place the dog in neutral, so to speak, and is useful when setting nets, conversing with the farmer or entering ferrets to the warren.

Heel!

The heel enables the ferreter to take his dog through farmyards and stock without it getting in the way of machinery or disturbing flighty livestock. A dog that follows you in a higgledy-piggledy fashion getting in the way of tractors and scattering sheep to the four winds will soon get you invited to leave the farmer's property. The amount of equipment that a ferreter has to carry will also mean that he will not want to have to wrestle with a dog that can only be walked on the lead.

Stay and Lie down!

These commands are often used in conjunction to place the dog in a certain position for an indeterminate or prolonged period of time. A good example of this is seen when a rabbiting dog is sited by a bolt hole that cannot be netted, where it should remain until it receives either another command or the rabbit bolts when it is

The Jack Russell in the sit position at a warren where she is deployed to guard a hole that cannot be netted.

quite permissible for the dog to function automatically.

In accord with the basic obedience training that a dog undergoes, the owner should endeavour to ensure that his charge receives sufficient and varying human and canine company so that the animal is confident and sociable in all situations. When my mongrel was a puppy I used to walk her where I knew she would meet other dogs and be fawned upon by children and adults alike. There is nothing worse than taking a growling teeth-baring fury onto somebody else's land which amounts to an abuse of their courtesy as well as undermining the ferreter's whole presentation of himself as a serious sportsman.

Advanced Training

Once the dog has achieved basic obedience, the handler can contemplate extending the animal's education and adding to its repertoire those skills that will make it without doubt a true countryman's dog. Our main concern with advanced training is to encourage the dog to behave appropriately when it is in the midst of livestock. Too many farmers have seen a disobedient rogue of a dog produce panic amongst their prized animals and are justifiably cautious about all dogs thereafter. Consequently, the ferreter's dog must learn to be sound with stock at an early age and learn the lesson well. Hand in hand with stock familiarization is the development of a relationship of respect or affection between dog and ferret so that they may successfully work together when out rabbiting. Just as a farmer would not tolerate a harum-scarum dog on his land, I find the suggestion of a dog that will harm ferrets as soon as the keeper's back is turned both ridiculous and impractical. No matter how many rabbits

Both dog and ferreter must be sensible around the livestock that they will inevitably encounter whilst out hunting.

Amongst the most common livestock are cattle, horses and sheep.

such a dog can catch it is no kind of ferreter's companion and has deficient training. It is quite a common trick to get a ferret and dog to share milk from the same bowl in an effort to develop a partisan spirit between the animals, but I have my doubts about this method mainly because a ferret will literally befriend the devil for a drink of milk and such friendship lasts only until the bowl becomes empty.

It is far better to build a real relationship of trust between your working animals which requires nothing more than time and supervision. Some suggest that ferret kits and canine puppies should be brought up together because

Now that I live in Wales I am encountering more sheep than I used to and a badly trained dog will soon scare and scatter the shepherd's flock.

by so doing they will become accustomed to each other's presence and purpose. However, my dog is on friendly terms with all my ferrets, although she did not share her puppyhood with any of them and, as with stock familiarization, I have found that the key to success is gradual and continual exposure. Before attempting to get a dog of any age used to different and maybe strange animals the keeper must make sure that he has a sure-fire way of stopping his dog from causing any injury if it becomes aggressive. Allow your dog to be by your side when you are watching ferrets loose exercise outside the shed and then progress after a week or two to taking the dog into the ferret shed. Praise the dog when it is playful, kind and pleasant with the ferrets; I use the command 'Gentle!' to check my dog from becoming overenthusiastic with her clod-hopping paws as she tries to elicit a dance from one of the ferrets. My brother uses the word 'Steady!' to hold back his feisty terrier from

unleashing her instincts and killing what she doubtlessly considers to be vermin. An appropriate command suffices for both dogs who can be left alone in a closed shed with twenty loose ferrets and not injure any of them. The dogs which will chase and kill wild rabbits, or perhaps I should state more accurately my dog will do the chasing and my brother's terrier the killing, cohabited, dare I say gladly, with the largest lop-eared rabbit ever seen called Gilbert. Gilbert used to hop about the house unhindered and even invaded the sanctum of the dog beds with no reprisals forthcoming. To learn what is legitimate prey and what should be left alone is one of the most important lessons for the ferreter's dog and is why stock familiarization is considered advanced training. Once the dog is used to ferrets, introduce it to your chickens, ducks and rabbits or whatever else you may have in your backyard.

When the dog is trustworthy with your own

A dog that is trustworthy with ferrets is essential and time should be taken to socialize the animals properly.

menagerie it is time to consider taking it down to the farm to meet some sheep, pigs, cows and horses. At first this should be practised with the dog on the lead. It should be praised for calm behaviour and checked by voice and a gentle tug on the lead at the earliest sign of any aggression. A dog that is not trustworthy with farmstock is a liability to the ferreter who will soon get asked to leave the farmer's land and so perseverance in this department is essential. When the dog has mastered walking through stock on the lead, then it is time for the ultimate test as the lead is removed and the dog required to accompany the owner without being distracted as he walks round fields occupied with farm animals. Both my mongrel and my brother's terrier can quarter the ground following the scent of a rabbit and moving through a herd of sheep

without causing undue disturbance. This is purely the result of prolonged exposure to farm stock.

Caution should be displayed regarding the farm stock to which the dog is exposed and those animals that are known to be aggressive avoided. I have known savage horses and cattle that have gone for and attacked dogs and in so doing destroyed the canines confidence and future prospects as a sporting companion.

To drop food or caught prey on command is a particularly useful trait in the working dog's character. It may save the dog from poisoning and enables the ferreter to remove a caught rabbit from the jaws of a keen canine and dispatch it without further ado. I have seen my brother's terrier fasten her grip on a rabbit and shake it like a rag doll until it is dead, but on

When training my dog how to behave around livestock I began at home by taking her with me around the chickens and as the picture shows she is totally trustworthy.

My brother taking the time and using the open space to introduce his dog to a confident ram.

The dog should pose no threat to livestock and here both cattle and dog remain calm.

those occasions when she comes across a large buck she is unable to kill it with acceptable speed and intervention must take place in order to prevent unnecessary suffering. This is when the command 'Drop it!' is most crucial. My brother got into the habit of getting his dog to relinquish her food and toys when she was a puppy and in similar manner can make her release a rabbit when it is imperative to interfere with her natural method of dispatch. I do not have this problem because a rabbit has to be dead before my mongrel will get hold of it.

Encouraging the Natural Instincts of the Working Dog

I believe the best way to encourage a puppy to utilize its natural instincts is to put it into the field with a more experienced animal, which is

The desired behaviour of the working dog that is responding wholly to the handler and taking no interest in the ram.

the way my mongrel learnt her craft from the businesslike and learned terrier. It is also the lesson of nature as, for example, a young stoat or weasel will be taught by the mother how to stalk and kill quarry. In like manner an immature Peregrine falcon is supervised by the parents until it can hunt successfully by itself.

If you are not fortunate enough to have a tutor in the shape of a tried and tested dog, then the task of encouraging the puppy's natural instincts becomes the task of the owner. In this endeavour, patience and observation are going to be the watchwords. The natural instincts of the dog are the force of its strongest senses that will impel its actions. The actions that the ferreter should encourage from his dog are when it follows the line or scent of the rabbit run, follows the scent to the warren and marks the

hole, pursues rabbits above ground and marks the warren into which they escape. The best way to develop such behaviour in your dog is to take it to a natural arena where its senses are enlivened such as a well-populated field of rabbits and allow the animal the space to act naturally rather than bombard it with specific instructions. Always remember to praise the dog without delay when it instinctively does those things that are going to be beneficial when out ferreting.

The Purpose of the Ferreting Dog

Essentially, the purpose of the ferreter's dog is to fill or help fill the bag with rabbits. It will do this by either catching rabbits on the surface or

The Jack Russell is probably the most popular rabbiting dog and one of its chief virtues is the ability to penetrate the dense undergrowth when working.

driving them below so that they can be ferreted. The most common use of my brother's wiry terrier is to act like a four-legged beater, probing dense undergrowth and flushing out hidden rabbits. Her short stature, broad chest and hefty weight make her ideal for this job and if she scents or sights a rabbit, nothing in the world will prevent her relentless pursuit. My mongrel, lacking the speed and instinct to catch and kill a rabbit in the open, will give chase and then mark the warren awaiting our arrival, and her keen eyesight and ability to accurately mark has enabled us to catch rabbits on the most difficult of grounds.

As my brother and I were out one day having a glorious time catching rabbits we noticed a substantial number of fat rabbits scurry to a huge burrow at the base of a mature cedar tree. On first inspection we could not see how we could net the holes that were annoyingly located under the outstretched branches of the cedar. Despite repeated efforts we could not squeeze our bodies under the low branches and rather peevishly turned to walk away when the little terrier gave us inspiration as she disappeared under the branches. Approximately six holes lay beyond the reach of the interfering branches and we eagerly netted them. The dogs needed no instructions and seemed to anticipate our objective. A well-behaved ferret was shoved along the ground and entered one of the holes that was not netted and nearest to the tree trunk. Seconds later, a rabbit bolted like lightning out of an unnetted hole heading for the open

A good example of the ferreter's dog marking a warren indicating that there are rabbits at home.

ground, but before it could break free from the cover of the branches both dogs intercepted forcing the rabbit swiftly back below the surface. This was to be repeated time and again and necessitated immense concentration on the part of our dogs. The rabbits were unwilling to stay below ground in the company of the fierce ferret and tried to bolt again, but this time they had

Desired Characteristics of the Rabbiting Dog

The dog must be:

Fundamentally obedient and responsive.

Trustworthy with livestock and ferrets.

Fit enough to endure an arduous day's hunting.

Calm and methodical when working.

Able to mark accurately

Able to penetrate undergrowth and work hedges.

Happy in its role.

Able to act instinctively.

moved nearer to the outskirts of their warren and were caught in the purse nets. At the conclusion of our endeavour we had accounted for five nice rabbits. Using the dogs in this way to guard unnetted holes and force rabbits back below the surface to emerge where you want them is a challenging task requiring well-behaved dogs, but it does mean that you can have success with warrens that would otherwise not be workable.

When working very large warren systems it is sometimes difficult to discern where the rabbit is going to bolt from. If you are too far removed from the scene of the action, the rabbit may disentangle itself from a poorly or hurriedly set net. However, if you observe the working dog, it will be noted that the animal is edging its way towards or inclining its head in the direction from which the rabbit is to bolt. Consequently, the craft of ferreting relies heavily upon the ferreter's ability to correctly read and interpret the behaviour of his animals. Sally, the mongrel, gives a vivid illustration of this because you can actually tell by her behaviour and gestures what type of scent she has picked up. If it is a rabbit, she will fasten her nose to the ground and she quarters back and forth, but if it is a fox the hair of her body and tail explode to attention as if she has been electrocuted; if on the other hand she stumbles upon the scent of a bird, she will stand silent and still pointing with upraised paw. To maximize the use of the dog in the field, quality time must be spent studying and interpreting the animal's behaviour. Listening to our dogs has not only reaped handsome rewards in the bagging of rabbits, but at times enabled us to retrieve ferrets which had exited the warren and were wandering about on the surface.

The joy of a good country dog is its ability to continually surprise by doing just what is needed at the exact time required and such an animal is without doubt worth its weight in gold. The pleasure derived from the training and company of such a dog is inestimable and every serious ferreter should have a good dog by his side.

10 ALTERNATIVE HUNTING METHODS

Digging

I am aware that when the ferreter encounters a warren from which the rabbits will not bolt he will resort to digging a hole to retrieve his ferret and any rabbits that it has killed or immobilized underground. The widespread use of locators and accuracy with which contemporary ferreters can conduct a dig has led me to conclude that digging is very much a hunting method in its own right. However, digging should never be a first, but rather a last resort because it disturbs the living environment of quarry that the hunter wants to see perpetuate itself in reasonable numbers.

In order to employ the digging method the ferreter must be able to pinpoint accurately the position of his ferret below ground and know how to dig down to it without causing any tunnels to collapse. A locator is the obvious tool of choice and is consistently reliable provided that time has been taken to acquaint oneself with its workings. Once the ferret is located and no longer on the move a round hole about a foot in diameter should be dug at the appropriate position. Care should always be taken to cut out the top turf so that it can be neatly replaced once the dig has been completed. After the turf is removed a long-handled spade is used to open up a long narrow hole down to the ferret. As the spade feels as if it is going to break through into the tunnel of the warren it should be exchanged for a trowel or the hand to clear away the thin final layer of soil and the ferret and rabbit upon which it is laid up should become visible.

Digging with the aid of the locator is efficient and increases the number of rabbits that is bagged, but is of little use in frosty sub-zero temperatures when the ground is as hard as cement. It is an activity which should also never be rushed into just because nothing seems to be happening in the warren and I have a recollection of my brother starting to dig furiously as his impatience got the better of him and when he had got about a foot down he turned round to see the albino hob standing behind him watching. I have read about and talked to other ferreters who have an aversion to digging and would rather sit down and have a flask of tea while they wait for a ferret to return and do not mind losing the odd rabbit that is killed below ground knowing that it will soon be recycled in the wild. Clearly, digging is a viable and fruitful option which is available to those with the right equipment and motivation.

Shooting to Ferrets

Why shoot rabbits bolted by a ferret when netting is obviously more effective? one may well ask. Shooting adds variety, is much quicker and is a real challenge for the most capable of guns. My brother who has been on many organized pheasant shoots as a beater is of the opinion that a bolted rabbit accelerating along the ground is far more difficult to hit than a high-flying pheasant.

If the intention is to use the technique of entering the ferret in conjunction with a shotgun for shooting the bolting rabbits, the ferret used must remain unperturbed when loud explosive noises occur. The best way to ensure that the ferret is aware that the sound of a gunshot poses no threat to it is to take the animal in a carrier where it can be observed and get somebody to release a few rounds while you assess its reactions and offer any necessary reassurance. Offer the ferret some milk and if it begins to drink, it is obvious that the loud noises are not unduly disturbing it. If the ferret is petrified, halt the proceedings immediately and reserve the animal for quieter sport.

There are basic rules that should be adhered to when shooting rabbits to ferrets and these are briefly outlined below:

1) Become a competent shot before contemplating this very challenging type of shooting.

2) Do not shoot any rabbit while it is still in the burrow because

   a. If you only wound the rabbit it will retreat back into the burrow beyond capture and humane dispatch.

   b. An injured rabbit will not bolt again and will not be able to evade the ferret for long, resulting in a lay up.

   c. When shooting a rabbit in a burrow it is not unknown for several pellets to completely pass the rabbit and fatally strike the ferret.

3) All rabbits should be in open ground before they are shot and an injured rabbit should be shot a second time to prevent a slow painful death.

4) Do not load a weapon until the ferret has been entered and the person doing the entering has reached a predetermined point that is well out of range. If the other person wishes to return to the field of fire he must first gain your permission and you must unload the shotgun before he approaches.

5) If two guns are being used it is imperative that each has a clearly defined arc of fire that is strictly adhered to.

If you intend to use guns you must make this plain to the owners of the land from whom you have gained permission and tell them on the day of the shoot where you will be working.

Ferrets and Birds of Prey

The use of raptors for the pursuit of quarry has a long and varied history that spans the centuries in similar fashion to ferreting, but is considered a bit more up-market. It is essentially hawks that are used for the pursuit of rabbits with falcons being flown at winged quarry. Rabbits provide good sport because they are fast and agile, but can be dangerous because of their powerful back legs. It is the size and power of a bird's feet combined with its agility on the wing that determine its prey and most hawks are a good match for a rabbit. Examples include the Common Buzzard and Goshawk which are both indigenous birds and hunt rabbits in the wild. The Red Tailed Buzzard and Harris Hawk which hail from the United States are also suitable. A hawk can never hope to catch as many rabbits as nets will, but the spectacle of watching a raptor in hot pursuit of its natural quarry will more than make up for a small bag.

There needs to be plenty of open ground if the hawk is to stand a chance of catching a rabbit which has been bolted by a ferret. Warrens close to cover or within easy reach of other warrens will stack the odds heavily in favour of the rabbits and render it virtually impossible for the hawk to make a kill. Hilly and mountainous grounds are ideal for a hawk, but the experienced hawker or 'austringer', to give him his correct title, can make the most of a bad job and use his bird in more enclosed country. Warrens that are small and compact should be chosen as a rabbit bolted from one of the large systems will have the option of re-entering an outlying hole once it senses the presence of an airborne predator.

It is possible for one person to go hunting alone with a good hawk and equally good ferret, but should anything go wrong he or she has no backup. It is far more sensible to go hawking as a pair with one person being responsible for the hawk and the other for the ferret.

Before going hunting with these animals the hawk should be trained to ferrets, and my brother's falconry instructor who is reputed to

*Using raptors is an ancient and spectacular way to hunt and an exciting option
for the entrepreneurial ferreter.*

be one of the finest falconers in the country suggested the following training method. First of all the ferret should be placed on a bed of straw and covered with a fish tank which has ventilation holes and is secured with a heavy rock on top of it. This should be set up within striking distance of the hawk's perch and the idea is that the hawk upon seeing the ferret will attack repeatedly, but be held at bay by the fish tank, and the ferret with customary prowess will curl up and go to sleep in the straw. He believed that if this process was repeated several times it would establish in the hawk's mind the conviction that the ferret is surrounded by some type of protective field and not worth attacking. By the completion of this training the hawk should simply ignore the presence of the ferret. Most austringers are of the opinion that an albino ferret is best for hawking because it is not easily mistaken for a rabbit and is a sensible precaution, for once the raptor is released it cannot be called off like a dog.

Whichever method of hunting with ferrets appeals to the reader, it should be remembered that it is the ferret that is pivotal to the success of each endeavour and it should be treated and rewarded appropriately.

11 THE SITUATION TODAY

A Popular Animal with Varied Uses

During previous years, the ferret has steadily increased in popularity – a fact that can be attributed to a desire to control recovering rabbit populations by a natural method and the realization that the ferret possesses a wealth of character that makes it appealing to keep.

Since ancient times the ferret has been in man's employ for the purpose of rabbit catching, but in our contemporary society there are a good number of people who keep ferrets that have never seen the inside of a warren, at which traditional fiedsports enthusiasts shake their heads in bewilderment and incredulity. However, it does make one wonder whether there are reasons for keeping a ferret other than the obvious one of hunting rabbits.

I discovered my own answer to this question when I had to relinquish my prized and productive rabbiting rights due to a change of location and was faced with the prospect of no hunting ground for the impending season. Even today I have not acquired access to the quality of land of my coveted rights of yesteryear. Firstly, one has to consider what other inherent capabilities the ferret possesses and how they can be made manifest for human benefit, and secondly assess the characteristics of the animal and ascertain whether its individuality and behaviour are reward enough for keeping it.

My late grandfather, a northern farm worker and market trader, had an impressive row of poultry and tool sheds adjacent to his highly productive vegetable garden and was forced to deal with the inevitable attention of rats that treated the underside of the shed floor as their sanctum. He owned a heeler called Trixie whom he expected to catch any rats that were exposed, but when he witnessed egg theft he decided to call in Dick Rigby and his notorious ferret. And so it was one Sunday morning that men gripping shovels and with bicycle clips fastening the bottom of their trousers surrounded the sheds in preparation for the hasty exit of rats from below. Women and children were confined to watch from the house as Dick approached holding within his gauntleted hands a stupendous ferret wearing a chain lead. Within moments of its feet touching the ground a scurry of rats began in diverse directions and those that evaded the shovels were caught by the ever-present Trixie, choosing to seal their fate above ground rather than face the gargantuan beast that had invaded their sanctum.

Once the business was completed Dick recovered his ferret, received a gratifying comment and was promised a helping hand and some vegetables when he needed them. Dick was a roughshooter and wildfowler who spent his spare time shooting on the marshes and consequently did not pursue rabbits with the ferret. His sole reason for keeping the ferret was as an agent of pest control. Some enthusiasts consider rat catching employing the ferret as not only a sport in its own right, but an exhilarating pastime without equal. Needless to say, such folk soon acquire friends and have no shortage of locations in which to practise their sport.

While instilling new life into the antiquated cottage roof of our previous abode, an elderly thatcher recounted tales of his young grandchildren and their exploits with a newly acquired ferret. The ferret was bought with the intention of keeping the lads occupied and introducing them to the concept and responsibility of animal husbandry. The grandfather had purchased a locator with which the grandchildren were able to follow the ferret's every move and play a simplistic form of hide and seek with the animal. As children mature the ferret will, without doubt, provide an avenue of introduction for them into the world of fieldsports.

A retired gardener who came to cast his inspecting eye over our poultry on a weekly basis related how his brother kept a ferret with which they would go rabbiting, but rarely if ever catch anything and this was in pre-myxomatosis days! Despite this his brother insisted on keeping the ferret, claiming that it gave him an interest outside the house and was part and parcel of country living.

Both tales relate valuable reasons for keeping a ferret that include education and interest, and a book dealing with incorporating animals in primary education even suggests that the ferret is an ideal creature for enlivening school lessons and facilitating learning. Animals are being increasingly utilized in diversional and rehabilitative therapy among people of all ages and abilities. I recently read an article about flying displays featuring owls held at schools, nursing and residential homes. These were enthusiastically received, and research in nursing has resulted in the acquisition of, or regular visitation by, cats and dogs to the long-term care of the elderly wards. Consequently, during the summer my brother and I explored the poten-

The ferrets are fundamental to my success as a rabbit catcher and make wonderful companions for the countryman.

tial of using the ferret to provide an uplifting or enjoyable experience for those with or without special needs. We found that the people, including those with learning disabilities, bored youngsters and the elderly, who visited our ferret shed were intrigued by the appearance and conduct of the ferrets who performed characteristic antics and manifested friendly behaviour for the benefit of their visitors.

The ferret is an ideal companion for the country dweller because of its ability to deal with pests and its responsiveness to human company. I keep ferrets predominantly for rabbiting, but they are available for controlling rat problems and provide me with pleasure and satisfaction on a daily basis as I busy myself with maintaining and inspecting their condition.

I have come to the conclusion that if, God forbid, I was never able to rabbit again, there remain worthwhile reasons for continuing to keep the spirited ferret. However, at the time of writing I am anticipating an active season of sport and hope to add to my pleasure by incorporating the use of a buzzard and a whippet into my rabbiting endeavours in the near future and will be recording carefully my progress and success with them.

The Appeal of Ferreting

The traditional use of the ferret to pursue rabbit continues to appeal to generations of country dwellers. This may be in part because it is a rural tradition combined with the growing interest in keeping alive old skills and pastimes. However, ferreting has the added fascination of observing the animals use their instinctive behaviour for a recognized and beneficial purpose. Since taking up the sport I have become a lot more knowledgeable about British wildlife and flora and am beginning to really see nature for what it is, despite having lived in the countryside for the greater part of my life. Without doubt I have acquired access to some beautiful locations purely because I am a fieldsportsman and just being at such sites is a pleasure in its own right.

Consequently, ferreting has for me become part and parcel of an entire way of life that is firmly founded in living off, enjoying and preserving the countryside and its customs.

There is always something to do for the ferreter who enjoys his animals and sport, and it is quite obvious which activities will interest him during the winter, but what about the long hot summer months? Hot weather combined with country wisdom has restricted the ferreter's hunting season with the resulting summer abstinence enabling the multiplication of quarry and eliminating the risk of heat-induced stress for the predator. However, the traditionalist who only rabbits when an 'r' occurs in a month is not faced with the tedium of inactivity longing for September to arrive and dreaming of memorable hunting endeavours of yesteryear. A host of chores and decisions to be completed and made in preparation for the forthcoming rabbit season make this period nearly as intensive as the season itself.

The first question that the ferret keeper needs to tackle relates to his present level of stock, their make-up and suitability for rabbiting. If one has a team of novice and established workers no further action is required, but if not, you need to decide which out of breeding or purchasing is the best option for introducing new blood. If a ferret keeper finds himself with a number of adult hobs from which he does not intend to breed, then summer is the time, due to the physiological changes that occur in the male, to consult the veterinary surgeon regarding the option of castrating the hitherto entire ferrets.

The fine summer weather allows the ferret the opportunity to spend the majority of its day exercising or in blissful sleep within the exercise run while efforts are made to rejuvenate its distressed home. My brother and I have found that routine annual maintenance tasks such as strengthening and disinfecting the litter corner all combine to improve the appearance of an ailing cage and prolong its use. Vital to the success of the ferreter's hunting exploits are the condition and quality of his equipment which must be in good repair and ready for use when September arrives. The best way to ensure this is to make an initial assessment of the equipment and its need for repair or renewal during the early summer months. In my case this often results in the making and mending of nets and purchase of clothing to replace worn-out garments. My ground clearance tools are kept sharp and functional as a result of being used throughout the summer on the vegetable plot. Visits to game and county shows are recommended for the seeker of bargains while the services of specialist mail order firms make every item available for the more reclusive ferreter.

As the urge to hunt becomes increasingly strong towards the end of the summer, the enthusiastic ferreter endeavours to secure new rabbiting rights and renew existing ones. Consequently, the summer is far from an idle time for the canny ferreter who, in addition to caring for his animals on a daily basis, thoughtfully prepares for the forthcoming rabbiting season and in so doing eliminates those obstacles that would distract him from and delay his progress in catching the rabbit. The fact that these preparations for successful working can be made during the summer is one of the great benefits of being a ferreter and facilitate continued interest in one of the passions of a countryman's life.

Is Ferreting Relevant in Our Contemporary Rural Environment?

Increasingly, farmers such as those dwelling in south-west Scotland are calling for a controlled response to rising rabbit numbers that in the area specified are being killed at a rate of around forty thousand a year. They claim that ten rabbits will consume what one breeding ewe requires and are justifiably counting the cost of the current rise in numbers. While none of the farmers with whom I have conversed would like to see a return to methods such as myxomatosis, they all agree that a measured response is necessary. The use of ferrets by the rabbit clearance societies of the 1950s and 1960s testifies to the relevance of using these creatures to address the current problem.

Wild rabbit is also becoming popular with gastronomes and should therefore be killed by a method that will allow the meat to enter the food industry. The butchers to whom I have spoken offer without exception the highest prices for ferreted rabbits. Ferreting is the ideal method for combining conservation with control and its continuance can be justified even when there is a great deal of public sentiment opposed to fieldsports. Although ferreting has experienced little change since it began 700 years ago it remains a relevant and useful technique for hunting the illustrious rabbit.

INDEX